About the Author

© 1995 Troy Freeman

Carol Jago has taught English at the middle and high school levels for 26 years. She also directs the California Reading and Literature Project at UCLA. Carol writes a weekly education column for the *Los Angeles Times* and has been published in numerous professional journals. She is the author of *Nikki Giovanni in the Classroom: "The same ol danger but a brand new pleasure"* (NCTE, 1999), and is the Editor *of California English.*

With Rigor for All

With Rigor for All

Teaching the Classics to Contemporary Students

CAROL JAGO

With a Foreword by James Strickland

Calendar Islands Publishers
Portland, Maine

Calendar Islands Publishers LLC
477 Congress Street, Portland, Maine 04101

First published by Calendar Islands Publishers, 2000

ISBN 1–893056–06–6

Library of Congress Cataloging-in-Publication Data
Jago, Carol, 1951–
    With rigor for all : teaching the classics to contemporary students /
    Carol Jago
    p. cm.
    Includes bibliographical references.
    ISBN 1–893056–06–6
    1. Literature—Study and teaching (Secondary)   2. Best books.
    I. Title.

PN59.J34 2000
820.9'00071'273—dc21

                                                              00–020665

Editor: James Strickland
Design by Phillip Augusta

Printed in the United States of America

05 04 03 02 01 00   10 9 8 7 6 5 4 3 2 1

"Read the best books first, or you may not have a chance to read them at all."

Henry David Thoreau

Contents

Foreword

I met Carol Jago in print long before I met her in person.

Early in my tenure as editor of the *English Leadership Quarterly* (in the days when it was known by the ungodly string of letters as the *CSSEDC Quarterly* (Conference of Secondary School English Department Chairs), I told an anecdote in one of my introductory essays about a conversation that took place during one of those big conference Secondary Section luncheons. The person next to me, between the main course and dessert, asked me, as a college professor, what high school English teachers could do to better prepare their students for college. I'm never ready for that type of question, though I suppose I should be. The advice I offered at the time was simple: stop teaching the term paper. After the issue came out that carried that particular editorial, I received a note from a teacher at Santa Monica High School in California, who wrote that she agreed with me, adding that she had already stopped teaching the traditional term paper. The note writer was Carol Jago. I wrote back and asked her to tell me more, suggesting that "Alternatives to the Term Paper" might make an interesting theme for an upcoming issue.

Carol responded. Her piece was short but powerful. In it she called the traditional term paper a "waste of time," and she proceeded to tell of an alternative research project that grew out of a reading her students enjoyed, Maxine Hong Kingston's *Woman Warrior*. Her students, it seems, were truly interested in finding out more about Chinese superstitions, so Carol taught them how real research was done. As an editor, a relatively new one at that, I performed what might be termed heavy editing on the piece—tightening and rearranging sentences and even whole paragraphs. I was worried that this stranger would yank the essay when she saw what I had done, as one member of my own English department had done, appalled that someone had dared to edit her prose. Instead, not only did Carol approve the changes, but she sent another manuscript, an essay explaining how she used the double entry journal, already a fixture in her classes, to interact with the student teacher she had agreed to mentor. I published that essay too, as quickly as I could.

Then I met Carol Jago in person, at the 1990 NCTE conference in Atlanta. She was every bit as lively as her prose, as enthusiastic as I pictured she must be in her classroom, and as friendly as though we'd gone to grammar school together. Before we knew it, we were talking about books. To say Carol is a voracious reader wouldn't begin to cover it. What I liked was that from that conference on I always left with a "must-read" title from Carol—and they've all been unusual but wonderful. I remember *Snow Falling on Cedars, Last Orders, The Woman Who Walked Into Doors,* and *The English Patient.* Twice I thought I found treasures to recommend to Carol—Ernest Gaines' *Lesson Before Dying* and Nick Hornby's *High Fidelity.* But Carol had already read them. I think Carol's students know she loves reading (there's no way to fake that); how else can you convince students to be readers if you're not a reader yourself?

Over the course of my six-year tenure as editor, I published nine of Carol's essays. Each piece required less and less editing as Carol developed into a master of the short essay. The highlight of our relationship was when the editorial board of the *English Leadership Quarterly* selected her essay, titled "No More Objective Tests, Ever," as the best article published in the *Quarterly* during 1992. As Carol says, "Take a moment to think about the last book you read. What stayed with you? It is probably neither the characters' names nor a short identification tag about them. What stayed with you is probably a feeling for the book, a message the author conveyed especially to you, a world you walked in for the period of time you read. How would you feel about taking a test on this story and answering true-or-false questions about what happened or what the book meant?

"I know such a test would severely undermine the pleasure I took from the latest book I read, José Saramago's *Blindness*. Although I finished the novel only yesterday, I could not with certainty tell you the main characters' names. Does this make me a poor reader? Should I be punished for remembering the haunting narrative voice rather than the name of the city where the story took place? Though I am itching to talk with someone about the book, I do not want to have to match my reading of it with anyone else's. For someone—anyone, even the author—to be set up as the arbiter of what a book says to a reader contradicts everything we know about reading. Why would I practice in my classroom that which I do not believe is true in the 'real' world?"

I presented her with the 1992 Outstanding Article award at the Fall 1993 NCTE in Pittsburgh. I was proud. I was proud of discovering an outstanding teacher; I was proud of my *Quarterly* publication that published her ideas; I was proud to know Carol Jago.

Today I'm even prouder.

Following the success she's enjoyed as editor of the *California English* journal and author of *Nikki Giovanni in the Classroom*, the first installment in a series on contemporary writers that she's begun for NCTE, Carol has written *With Rigor for All*, and she's allowed me to be her editor once again.

Carol takes chances. She lets her students compare the monster in *Beowulf* to the speaker in Tupac Shakur's rap songs. She lets her students do a "beat poetry" take on Odysseus' plight. She's welcomed the "pull-out" kids back into her classroom. She's challenged students to memorize poetry of their own choosing. She's allowed students to bring in poetry that speaks to them.

Don't let the brevity of this volume fool you. The stories Carol tells and the advice she offers are concentrated. Her ideas and strategies will fill your thoughts and the possibilities will multiply. You will see that what she's done with her students in Santa Monica can be done with your students and your curriculum. More important, you will see that the type of curriculum we reserve for the high-track students—those gifted, blessed, and chosen—can be offered for all. Without watering down the curriculum. Without "black and yellow" notes. Without remedial instruction. Carol's not teaching the "classics" so that her students can play the cultural literacy trivial pursuit game; she believes in the power of literature. She believes that "All books are not created equal. Some have the power to transport us to unexplored worlds and allow us—at least for as long as the book lasts—to become other than who we are. Others only ever attempt to offer us chicken soup for our teenage or middle-aged souls. While there is no question that it is easier to persuade students to pick up the second kind of novel, a critical reading of classical literature results in a deep literacy that I believe is an essential skill for anyone who wants to attempt to make sense of the world."

Carol's classroom resonates with Louise Rosenblatt's notion that the study of literature should be at the center of every child's life. "For most students, for most readers of any age, what is most important is the human experience that literature presents." And as keepers of the flame, it is our job to share that experience with our students . . . with rigor . . . and with all of them. Carol's book will inspire you; it will give you confidence. It's important; it's for the children.

JAMES STRICKLAND

Acknowledgments

Many thanks are due to Jim Strickland and Peter Stillman without whose support and guidance this book would never exist. I want also to thank Alfie Kohn for permission to reprint the *California English* interview which is copyright © 1995 by Alfie Kohn, and Simon & Schuster for permission to reprint excerpts from David Denby's *The Great Books*, copyright © 1996 by David Denby.

Finally, I must thank my students whose sparkling eyes and ready smiles make my work as a teacher such pleasure.

CAROL JAGO

Introduction

Rushed as I always am to get out of the house and on the road to school, I could not resist the morning paper's headline: "Something Is Rotund in Denmark." The story that followed was a rather dull article about poor eating habits in Denmark that was not a subject I typically found myself much drawn to. I began to wonder if the editor had created the headline in order to catch readers just like me.

While there weren't likely to be many *Los Angeles Times* readers who would be teaching *Hamlet* later in the day, it did seem that the editor counted on the fact that most people scanning the headlines would vaguely remember the ghost of Hamlet's murdered father and Marcellus proclaiming at the end of act 1, scene 4, that "Something is rotten in the state of Denmark."

I was eager to show the newspaper to my students. Here was one more bit of evidence proving that reading classical literature is not a punishment but a reward.

As an English teacher in a public urban high school, I know first-hand the challenges involved in teaching classical literature to today's students. One third of the 3,200 students at Santa Monica High School do not speak English at home. More than twenty different languages are spoken on campus. Our student body includes teenages who live in million-dollar homes and others who reside in homeless shelters.

Without powerful stories to engage them, many of these students will never acquire the literacy skills they need. I believe that the most potent stories are those that have weathered the test of time: the "classics."

Though most high school course descriptions still call for a heavy dose of classical literature, teachers (particularly teachers who care a great deal about making school meaningful) seem increasingly reluctant to tackle these works. Thinking that contemporary novels will be more accessible and less daunting for reluctant readers, they abandon *Great Expectations* for more contemporary stories. They wheel out the VCR and show Leonardo DiCaprio as Romeo rather than have students read and listen to Shakespeare's lines and perform the role for themselves. While young adult literature and big-screen adaptations most certainly have a place in the reading and viewing lives of today's teenagers, the work of a literature classroom should be the careful and joyful reading of challenging texts.

It seems criminal to me that schools should reserve the classics for honor students. Ignoring the elitism that such a curricular decision betrays, teachers defend a watered-down reading list for "regular" students by explaining to themselves and others that most teenagers simply can't understand the difficult vocabulary. Besides, they argue, today's kids won't read anything that is old. If Shakespeare or Dickens had operated from such an elitist stance, neither would have been the popular success he was. "Regular" people loved Shakespeare's and Dickens' works. Their contemporary audiences did so for the very same reasons that readers today laugh with Falstaff and cry with Little Nell. Shakespeare and Dickens make characters come alive. While caught up in the spell of the story, readers care about them the way they care about real people, worrying when the characters are in trouble, celebrating when they triumph.

I worry that in our determination to provide students with literature they can "relate to" we sometimes end up teaching works that students actually don't need much help with at the expense of teaching classics that they most certainly do need assistance negotiating. This is not to suggest that we stop putting contemporary literature into students' hands, but only to remind ourselves that we should be teaching in what Lev Vygotsky (1962) calls the zone of proximal development. He has written that "the only good kind of instruction is that which marches ahead of development and leads it" (104). If students can read a book on their own, it probably isn't the best choice for classroom study. Classroom texts should pose intellectual challenges to young readers. These texts should be books that will make students stronger readers—and stronger people.

When former students come to visit, I often see reflected in their eyes the question, "How could you still be doing the same old things after all this time?" Too polite to ask, they hint in subtle ways, fingering my ratty copy of *The Odyssey*, recognizing familiar assignments on the board. They can't quite believe that during all the time their lives have been changing so dramatically, mine has stayed the same. Or so they assume.

What I find impossible to explain to them is that while external things might remain the same, the students make it different every time around. For example, I would have thought that in twenty-five years I had seen every possible variation on a presentation of Book XIX of *The Odyssey*. But this year tenth grader Miguel Sawaya wrote what Book XIX might have sounded like had Homer been a beat poet:

Odyshus (sic)
    back
        standing in his conquered doorway
   and the sight of Penelope
        like Athene's creation of tangible ecstasy,
   and the suitors
        have eyes
        and weak knees

---

and burning towers for her.
> dreaming of naked breakfast
>> naked lunch
>> naked dinner

This beauty now speaks
> that her son's beard is sprouting
> and with it sprouts
>> her need for a new man
>> but the one with the greatest gifts;
> and the suitors,
>> in hysterics,
>> insatiable,
> lay their best treasures at her feet
while Odyshus is hip to the jive
> and the scene
> and digs his old lady
>> like never before.

I feel sorry for people who don't get to be English teachers. Each new group of students makes familiar texts come alive for me in new ways. Like Miranda when she first saw the likes of young men, I cannot help but exclaim, "Oh, brave new world that has such people in 't" (*The Tempest*, act 5, scene 1).

Apart from a rare few, the young people I teach do not pick up classic literature with much enthusiasm. At first they groan, "Three hundred pages of poetry!" Then they moan, "I can't do it. Not one word of what I read last night makes sense." They always hope that if they complain enough, I will abandon the text for something simpler. Instead I assure them that over the next few weeks I am going to show them how to unlock this book for themselves. I let students know that the satisfaction they will feel at meeting this textual challenge is an intellectual reward that I would not for the world deny them. Does every student experience this reward with every book?

Of course not. But many students who never expected to be able to negotiate classical literature find that with a little help from their teacher and classmates, the book isn't as impossible as they first thought. This dawning realization is an important instructional goal. Students are learning not to fear complicated syntax or unfamiliar vocabulary. As a result their literacy is enhanced.

Another goal I consciously pursue is love and respect for literature. In her provocative essay "I Know Why the Caged Bird Cannot Read," Francine Prose (1999) argues that:

> Traditionally, the love of reading has been born and nurtured in high school English class—the last time many students will find themselves in a roomful of people who have all read the same text and are, in theory, prepared to discuss it. High school—even more than college—is where literary tastes and allegiances are formed; what we read in adolescence is imprinted on our brains as the dreamy notions of childhood crystallize into hard data. (76)

Who knows but that without determined high school English teachers, love and respect for literature would die out. Not many students stumble upon the works of Thomas Hardy on their parents' bookshelves or choose to peek between the covers if they do. But for as long as teachers continue to make enduring stories come to life for young readers, the study of literature will remain a vital pursuit.

My definition of a classic is both vague and generous. A classic is an enduring story. As a result, the texts I use in my classroom include both works from antiquity and contemporary novels. I see no contradiction with placing Zora Neale Hurston's heroine Janie Crawford side by side with Homer's hero Odysseus. Both embark on journeys that lead to self-discovery. Both return home to tell those they have left behind what they learned. It is important that students don't mistakenly come to believe that "classic" is synonymous with "ancient." Classics are stories that tell the truth about human experience across both time and culture.

Given so many teenagers' reluctance to read at all, handing out a Shakespeare play or Homer's epic poem (let alone *Moby Dick* or *Crime and Punishment*) may seem like folly for both teacher and student. Living as we do in an age that glorifies the screen rather than the printed page, it can be very hard work to persuade young people to turn off MTV and pick up a book. What follows will attempt to dispel the fear of teaching classical texts to contemporary kids and offer ideas for helping young people learn to read these enduring stories.

CHAPTER ONE

Creating a Context for the Study of Classical Literature

All books are not created equal. Some have the power to transport us to unexplored worlds and allow us—at least for as long as the book lasts—to become other than who we are. Others only ever attempt to offer us chicken soup for our teenage or middle-aged souls. While there is no question that it is easier to persuade students to pick up the second kind of novel, a critical reading of classical literature results in a deep literacy that I believe is an essential skill for anyone who wants to attempt to make sense of the world.

Marshall Gregory (1997), Harry Ice Professor of English at Butler University, Indiana, posits six contributions that the study of literature makes to student development:

1. Students develop **intellectually** as the content of great works of literature offers them the ways and means of delving into stories, and, through these stories, of having a vicarious experience of the human condition far greater than any of them could ever acquire on the basis of luck and firsthand encounters.

2. Students develop **cognitive skills** through the study of literature that support the critical reading of all texts, the

precise use of language, and the creation of sound arguments.

3. Students develop an **aesthetic sensitivity** that helps them recognize and respond to art.

4. Students develop both an **intra and intercultural awareness** by reading texts both from their own culture and from cultures other than their own.

5. Students develop an **ethical sensitivity** that includes both the ability to regulate conduct according to principles and the ability to deliberate about issues both in their own heads and in dialogue with others.

6. Students develop an **existential maturity** that allows them to behave as civilized human beings in a world where others are not always so inclined. According to Gregory, existential maturity "is more easily defined by what it is not than by what it is. It is not self-centeredness; it is not unkindness; it is not pettiness; it is not petulance; it is not callousness to the suffering of others; it is not backbiting or violent competitiveness; it is not mean-spiritedness; it is not dogmatism or fanaticism; it is not a lack of self-control; it is not the inability ever to be detached or ironic; it is not the refusal to engage in give-and-take learning from others; it is not the assumption that what we personally desire and value is what everyone else desires and values." (57)

Literature Versus Workplace Documents

When the study of literature can accomplish so much (and so much that law enforcement and social services struggle in vain to accomplish), it seems foolhardy for schools to shortchange this essential element of a child's education. Yet all over this country curriculum experts are recommending that teachers focus on what they are calling workplace documents, influenced no doubt by a business community fed up with employees who need intensive and therefore expensive training before they can be put to work. Business leaders want schools to guarantee that graduates have workplace literacy, and in fact most state standards recommend that students learn to read with comprehension instruction manuals, consumer documents, and business memos. Standardized assessment instruments increasingly reflect these standards, and as assessment increasingly drives instruction, I fear there will be little time left in the curriculum for literature.

The cost of such a shift would be catastrophic. Elite private and suburban schools are not likely to replace *The Scarlet Letter* with workplace documents. The sons and daughters of the privileged will continue to read *The Odyssey* and *Beowulf* while urban public school kids are handed instruction manuals and consumer reports. A democracy isn't supposed to work this way.

Odysseus's adventures offer all teenage readers a useful map for internal navigation. If informational texts come to replace the classics in our curriculum, high schools will graduate young people who have never seen Circe turn men into swine, who have never sailed past Scylla and Charybdis, and who have no knowledge of the dangers lurking in the Land of the Lotus Eaters. If they never read the classics, students will truly be at sea.

And what is more "real world" than the story of *Beowulf?* A king is hounded by a seemingly all-powerful enemy and has no idea why this monster has singled out his land for destruction. Every night the evil beast creeps into his hall and slaughters the best and the brightest of his men. To survive, the men must abandon their leader and find safety in hiding. Despair reigns throughout the land until the arrival of—you guessed it—Beowulf.

Luring Students to the Text

One of the worst mistakes a teacher can make when introducing a classic like *The Odyssey* or *Beowulf* to students is to take the cod liver oil approach: "Drink this. It tastes bad, but it's good for you. You'll thank me later." Abandon all hope of instructional success if you pursue this course. First, the concept of suffering now for later pleasure is lost on most teenagers. And second, most kids I know are very good at just saying, "No."

Before I ever put *Beowulf* in students' hands, I tell them about Grendel and his penchant for human flesh. I paint them a picture of the egomaniac Beowulf—a man able to swim in the North Sea for nine days without rest, dressed in full chain mail and carrying a large sword. Swimmers in class become particularly intrigued. Their experience with the ocean tells them that this is simply impossible. Who is this guy? Or, who does this guy Beowulf think he is?

One Danger with Reading Aloud to Students

Once students have some sense of the story they will be reading— and one hopes a smattering of interest in the tale—I begin reading the epic aloud. A gifted reader, whether the teacher who knows the text well or a recording or an actor like Ian McKellen reading Robert Fagles' translation of *The Odyssey,* can make the words on the page come alive for students.

The problem with reading aloud, however, is that too often it is used to the exclusion of other methods for getting through a text. Unless the purpose of the lesson is a celebration of language for a kind of "read-in," teachers should not read whole works of literature aloud to their students. Reading aloud has become a popular teaching method for many of the wrong reasons: not having enough copies of a book to send home with students; students' poor reading skills; students' refusal to do homework. As a result, students are doing very little reading. Only a few pairs of eyes follow along in the text as the teacher reads aloud. Instead of eyes on the page, students are staring out the window. Yes, the classroom is quiet and the lesson seems productive. A principal passing by the classroom door would think, "My, what a good teacher." But the only one whose reading is improving is the teacher.

Given this caveat, I almost always begin a classic by reading aloud a few pages to my students. My voice helps bring sense to the unfamiliar text and, I hope, creates a model for the voice students will hear inside their heads as they read on their own. This opening gambit seems particularly appropriate for epic poetry. Since the works were created to be heard, it makes good sense for students being introduced to the poem to begin with the spoken word.

When I take up my imaginary lyre and begin reading *Beowulf*, I feel as though I am encouraging my students to perform daring intellectual deeds, take up a heroic challenge, slay their personal Grendel, and bring honor to their people. It is a tall order, but most teenagers seem to have plenty of time on their hands and more energy than they know what to do with. What they don't have is focus. For all Beowulf's shortcomings, no one could ever say he lacked focus. One has only to hear a few lines of Burton Raffel's translation of Beowulf's opening speech to become caught up in his character:

Hail, Hrothgar!
Higlac is my cousin and my king; the days
Of my youth have been filled with glory. Now Grendel's
Name has echoed in our land: sailors
Have brought us stories of Herot, the best of all mead-halls,
    deserted and useless when the moon
Hangs in skies the sun had lit,
Light and life fleeing together.

My people have said, the wisest, most knowing
And best of them, that my duty was to go to the Danes'
Great king. They have seen my strength for themselves,
Have watched me rise from the darkness of war,
Dripping with my enemies' blood. I drove
Five great giants into chains, chased
All of that race from the earth. I swam
In the blackness of the night, hunting monsters
Out of the ocean, and killing them one
By one; death was my errand and the fate
They had earned. Now Grendel and I are called
Together, and I've come.

Epic Poetry as a Site Where Things Happen

In an article titled "Reconceiving *Beowulf*: Poetry as Social Praxis,"
John D. Niles (1998), Professor of English at the University of California, Berkeley, explores the impact of epic poetry on contemporary readers:

> Oral poetic performances are often known for their magnificent
> displays of technical skill. Perhaps more importantly, however,
> they constitute a praxis affecting the way people think and act.
> The occasions of oral poetry provide a site where things happen,
> where power is declared or invoked, where issues of importance
> in a society are defined and contested. Oral poetry consists of
> creative acts whereby a mental order is produced or reaffirmed
> or one order is substituted for another. (143)

I would like to imagine that my reading of the first two hundred lines of *Beowulf* is a "magnificent display of technical skill," but however flawed it may be, it does seem to "provide a site where things happen."

When I asked my students to comment on Professor Niles' assertion in terms of the poetic performance of the singer in King Hrothgar's hall, tenth grader Nicole Chu wrote, "When the poet sings, he stresses the importance of war and victory in Hrothgar's society. Power is declared and the poet invokes men to fight for glory and fame. He reshapes the bloodshed and killings to fit the mold of an ideal society. The poet is doing something really important here because he builds up everyone's courage to do more daring deeds."

Nicole has gone to the heart of the matter. The first purpose of an epic poem is to entertain, to tell a story. But close at the heels of pleasure is the message that no careful listener can avoid. We, too, must define and contest the "issues of importance" for our own society. We, too, must become heroes.

Niles goes on to explain that:

> Works like the Homeric poems or *Beowulf* are not just cultural items to stuff into one's suitcase, "great books" to be checked off a list of things to know. In their manifold reiterations, whether in public performance or private reading, whether they are granted patronage by the great or find a more humble welcome, they involve the collaboration of many individuals. They are the result of a collective even restive engagement with the question of what wisdom is in a world that may seem stable or may seem in risk of spinning out of control. (160)

Inevitably our discussion of a world at risk of "spinning out of control" leads to the comparison of epic poetry with rap music. My students speak eloquently and can quote exhaustively from rap lyrics that they assert are today's epic poems. They are articulate in their defense of this art form as their generation's contribution to the oral tradition.

Tenth grader Dannell drew the class's attention to a passage in *Beowulf,* the one in which Grendel is first introduced:

13

A powerful monster, living down
In the darkness, growled in pain, impatient
As day after day the music rang
Loud in that hall, the harp's rejoicing
Call and the poet's clear songs, sung
Of the ancient beginnings of us all, recalling
The Almighty making the earth, shaping
These beautiful plains marked off by oceans,
Then proudly setting the sun and moon
To glow across the land and light it;
The corners of the earth were made lovely with trees
And leaves, made quick with life, with each
Of the nations who now move on its face. And then
As now warriors sang of their pleasure:
So Hrothgar's men lived happy in his hall
Till the monster stirred, that demon, that fiend,
Grendel, who haunted the moors, the wild
Marshes, and made his home in a hell
Not hell but earth. He was spawned in that slime,
Conceived by a pair of those monsters born
Of Cain, murderous creatures banished
By God, punished forever for the crime
Of Abel's death.

Then Dannell asked the class to compare that with the lyrics of Tupac Shakur. He played for the class "Words of Wisdom" from the album *2Pacalypse Now*. He then asked us to note the way Tupac describes himself in these lyrics. He calls himself "America's nightmare," whose purpose is to remind the oppressors what they have done to the oppressed. He says, just as Grendel did, that society should be afraid of him because he intends to revenge "four hundred plus years" of mistreatment. Tupac warns that we should be running from him and should be trying to silence him.

It was an uncanny moment, disconcerting for a teacher intent upon instilling traditional values and uncomfortable with gangsta rap. Still, there was powerful learning going on here. Dannell had seen the existential unfairness of Grendel's position. What had Grendel done to be cast as the monster? Even before reading John Gardner's novel *Grendel*, this student sympathized with the monster and recognized the barbarity within Hrothgar's "civilized" world. Not bad reading for a fifteen-year-old.

Intrigued by the possibilities Dannell's presentation suggested, I typed in "Tupac + Shakur + lyrics" into an Internet search engine to see what else I might find. All the lyrics to any of Tupac's songs are within reach of your fingertips. The more I read the more I was reminded of the lines in *Beowulf* where Grendel "snatched up thirty men, smashed them / Unknowing in their beds and ran out with their bodies, / The blood dripping behind him, back / To his lair, delighted with his night's slaughter." Hrothgar "wept, fearing / The beginning might not be the end."

Comparing Epic Poetry and Rap Lyrics

In class, we discussed the underlying ideas about violence, about exclusion, about love that both the anonymous author of *Beowulf* and the hip-hop superstar Tupac Shakur expressed. This was a heterogeneous group of tenth-grade students, some already college-bound in their minds, others more intent upon getting through high school with as little effort as possible. Dannell, for example, was failing every class he was enrolled in apart from English but was enormously self-confident. Popular and handsome, this African American young man strolled in late to class with a girl on each arm. Charles, on the other hand, was extremely gifted. But for all his intellectual prowess, he always seemed clueless when it came to getting along with his peers. In almost every classroom conversation, Charles managed to offend someone and as a result had a hard time getting others to hear what he had to say. Both Melinda and Nicole were outspoken young women, fearless when it came to standing up for their opinions.

Melinda: Grendel kills because that's what he was born to do. Sure it's gross to read, but he's a monster and monsters kill. Besides I'll bet one of the reasons people still read *Beowulf* is for the bloody parts.

Charles: Well, I don't think it's fair. In fact, the whole story of Cain and Abel bothers me. Cain killed Abel because God turned his back on his vegetables or something. All Grendel did wrong was to be born one of Cain's descendants. That sucks.

Nicole: Yeh, it sucks but that doesn't make it right for Grendel to kill innocent sleeping men.

Dannell: Not right but I can see why he does it. To me, Grendel's life is a lot like the life Tupac raps about. I mean, when Tupac says that society made him what he is, he's saying that when everybody who sees you hates you, you start to hate back, and when all you know is hate, killing feels natural.

Me: But that doesn't make the killing a virtue, does it? I hate the way rappers glorify violence.

Charles: No, but I'm with Dannell here. If I grew up all hairy and ugly like Grendel and never had anyone to teach me any different maybe I'd start having soldiers for lunch too.

Melinda: That's sick.

Me: Wait, think about what Charles is saying, Melinda.

Suddenly any need for a defense of classical literature as relevant to contemporary lives evaporated. Clearly some issues just don't change all that much across the centuries.

Marshall Gregory's Defense for the Study of Literature

Thinking about Marshall Gregory's defense of the study of literature, I saw that in their reading of *Beowulf* my students really had
developed intellectually. Many had never before met a hero like
Beowulf, so utterly sure of himself and his mission. Unlike a modern hero, Beowulf admits to no weaknesses nor does he succumb to
the temptations of ordinary life. While this made him an unrealistic character for some students, most were able to see how Beowulf's
exploits were not meant to be realistic, not for the epic poet's listeners any more than for readers like us. At the same time, students
were able to experience vicariously what it felt like to do battle with
a series of monsters: Grendel, Grendel's mother, and finally (fatally)
the dragon without ever giving up or giving in to self-doubt.

As they compared the epic poem to rap lyrics, these students
developed cognitive skills. Dannell and others could tell that I was
reluctant to accept the comparison and so had to examine carefully the ways in which both texts used language in order to support their claim. While I remain convinced that *Beowulf* is the ar-
tistically superior poem, a great deal of powerful classroom
discussion was triggered by the inclusion of Tupac Shakur's lyrics
in our lesson. And though it had not been Dannell's intention to
do so, he had developed in the rest of us a sense of what it means
to be an outsider in Hrothgar's land and in our own society. He
helped us begin to understand the rage that such a position can
engender.

Aesthetic and ethical sensitivity is hard to measure. So is ethical
maturity. But I believe that these tenth graders are well on their
way to developing the habits of mind Marshall Gregory describes.
Beowulf taught them things they didn't know they knew. Great books
will do that if you only give them a chance. Lesser books, while
excellent fare for pleasure reading, seldom have this kind of impact.

I don't teach the classics to help kids get into good colleges and secure high-paying positions in business and industry. I teach the classics because I believe these enduring stories provide nourishment for growing minds. Long after they have forgotten the teenage romances and science fiction they gobbled up, *Beowulf* will still inhabit a place in their minds.

What follows is a list of classics, both ancient and modern, that we use in the English department at Santa Monica High School. It is by no means set in stone. In fact, I have no doubt that in the interval between my writing this and your reading it, the list will have undergone several more incarnations. We are constantly looking for new titles worthy of close textual study that will engage reluctant readers, particularly ninth- and tenth-grade boys. As is the case in so many urban public high schools, many students never make it to the upper grades. We struggle to kindle a love for enduring stories in students in the hope that one teacher or one book can make a difference. Our search often results in the movement of titles from one grade level to another. What happens is that a particular teacher will get a good idea for a new thematic unit and need to work with what is available in the textbook room.

We have agreed that teachers may pick and choose from the department list as long as students at each grade level study at least one book as a class during each six-week grading period. During that period, students must also read a book of their own choosing. We negotiate who will get which book when on the day before school opens. For new teachers, this is obviously less than ideal. Eleventh-grade American Literature teachers who wish to teach a chronological course often use one of several sets of anthologies we have in the textbook room to supplement the novels. We also use various poetry anthologies: *Cool Salsa,* edited by Lorri Carlson; *Sound and Sense,* edited by Laurence Perrine; *The Vintage Book of Contemporary American Poetry,* edited by J. D. McClatchy; *The Vintage Book of Contemporary World Poetry,* edited by J. D. McClatchy. Our list of books is far from perfect and reflects years of inadequate funding for textbooks in California. We like to keep a department "wish list" at hand in case increased funding becomes available or a rich alumnus decides to reach for his checkbook. Some day in a just world, teachers will have all the money they need for books.

Classics by Grade Level
Santa Monica High School
Santa Monica, California

9th Grade

Great Expectations, Charles Dickens
Romeo and Juliet, William Shakespeare
Midsummer Night's Dream, William Shakespeare
Le Morte D'Arthur, Thomas Mallory
Metamorphosis, Franz Kafka
The Human Comedy, William Saroyan
The Doll's House, Henrik Ibsen
Night, Elie Wiesel
Hiroshima, John Hersey
The Sound of Waves, Yukio Mishima
Fahrenheit 451, Ray Bradbury
The Bluest Eye, Toni Morrison
The House on Mango Street, Sandra Cisneros
This Boy's Life, Tobias Wolff

10th Grade

Beowulf
The Odyssey, Homer
Julius Caesar, William Shakespeare
Twelfth Night, William Shakespeare
Much Ado About Nothing, William Shakespeare

The Stranger, Albert Camus
Brave New World, Aldous Huxley
Frankenstein, Mary Shelley
Lord of the Flies, William Golding
All Quiet on the Western Front, Erich Maria Remarque
A Separate Peace, John Knowles
The Heart Is a Lonely Hunter, Carson McCullers
The Catcher in the Rye, J. D. Salinger
The Chosen, Chaim Potok
Black Boy, Richard Wright
Bless Me, Ultima, Rudolfo Anaya
The Joy Luck Club, Amy Tan
Grendel, John Gardner
Woman Warrior, Maxine Hong Kingston
Chronicle of a Death Foretold, Gabriel García Márquez

11th Grade

The Scarlet Letter, Nathaniel Hawthorne
Huckleberry Finn, Mark Twain
Moby Dick, Herman Melville
The Red Badge of Courage, Stephen Crane
The Bear, William Faulkner
Walden and Other Writings, Henry David Thoreau
The Great Gatsby, F. Scott Fitzgerald
Death of a Salesman, Arthur Miller
The Crucible, Arthur Miller
The Night of the Iguana, Tennessee Williams
Of Mice and Men, John Steinbeck
Grapes of Wrath, John Steinbeck
A Raisin in the Sun, Lorraine Hansberry
Their Eyes Were Watching God, Zora Neale Hurston
In Our Time, Ernest Hemingway
A Farewell to Arms, Ernest Hemingway

The Sun Also Rises, Ernest Hemingway
Native Son, Richard Wright
I Know Why the Caged Bird Sings, Maya Angelou
Beloved, Toni Morrison
The Piano Lesson, August Wilson
Fences, August Wilson
Yellow Raft on Blue Water, Michael Dorris
The Color Purple, Alice Walker
Slouching Towards Bethlehem, Joan Didion
Jasmine, Bharati Mukherjee
Ordinary Love & Good Will, Jane Smiley

12th Grade

The Epic of Gilgamesh
The Oedipus Plays, Sophocles
Hamlet, William Shakespeare
King Lear, William Shakespeare
Henry V, William Shakespeare
Othello, William Shakespeare
As You Like It, William Shakespeare
The Tempest, William Shakespeare
The Merchant of Venice, William Shakespeare
Candide, Voltaire
Waiting for Godot, Samuel Beckett
Lord Jim, Joseph Conrad
Heart of Darkness, Joseph Conrad
Crime and Punishment, Fyodor Dostoevsky
The Trial, Franz Kafka
The Plague, Albert Camus
Things Fall Apart, Chinua Achebe
Rosencrantz and Guildenstern Are Dead, Tom Stoppard
Siddhartha, Hermann Hesse
On the Road, Jack Kerouac

One Flew Over the Cuckoo's Nest, Ken Kesey
The Things They Carried, Tim O'Brien
The Autobiography of Malcom X, Alex Haley
The Remains of the Day, Kazuo Ishiguro
The Left Hand of Darkness, Ursula Le Guin
Ceremony, Leslie Marmon Silko

In his essay "The Ethics of Teaching Literature," Wayne Booth (1998) has a section called "Why English Teachers, If They Teach Stories Ethically, Are More Important to Society Than Even the Best Teachers of Latin or Calculus or History." Booth's point is that literature is central to the education of every child. He asserts, and I fully agree, that it is through stories that students learn to confront ethical dilemmas. "Our most powerful ethical influences—except perhaps for parental modeling—are stories: it is in responding to, taking in, becoming transported by story that character is formed, for good or ill" (48).

Teaching the classics isn't easy, but it is most certainly important work. And isn't that why we went into this business in the first place?

CHAPTER TWO

Warning Students of the Obstacles in Reading Classics

In his 1987 Nobel Prize acceptance speech, Joseph Brodsky explained that

> In the history of our species, the book is an anthropological de-
> velopment, similar essentially to the invention of the wheel. Hav-
> ing emerged in order to give us some idea not so much of our
> origins as of what the Sapiens is capable of, a book constitutes a
> means of transportation through the space of experience, at the
> speed of turning a page.

The challenge for most teachers as they contemplate assigning a classic is how to help students operate this curious means of transportation and how to get them turning those pages. Judging from their commitment to literature, English teachers seem to agree that taking the textual trip through "the space of experience" is essential. What we struggle with is figuring out how to keep young readers moving.

"My students won't read anything longer than two hundred pages." "The vocabulary in Dickens is just too hard." "Description turns ninth graders off. They like action." "The print is too small." "It takes too long to get through." There is always a good reason for not doing something difficult. But we owe it to our young people to stop making excuses. We have to teach them how to read a classic.

Even excellent teenage readers are daunted by the textual challenges posed by a Jane Austen or Joseph Conrad novel. It is easy for English teachers to forget this. Often we know a text so well that it is hard to imagine what students might find confusing. Can you remember the first Shakespeare play you tried to read on your own? Do you recall your first time through *The Sound and the Fury* or *Lord Jim?* Did you or did you not resort to Cliffs Notes? Have you actually ever finished reading *Tristam Shandy* from cover to cover? I am not trying to make you feel guilty but to remind you that while you may be an expert reader, you weren't always one.

Experienced teachers often have read a play or novel that they teach anywhere from five to twenty-five times. The first time may have been in high school, the second in college, and once they began teaching, every year hence. I am quite sure I have read *Julius Caesar* at least twenty-two times. Given our own repeated exposure, it's easy to overlook just how difficult the book we place in teenagers' hands really is. And the first forty pages are typically the toughest.

How Teachers' Rereadings Can Interfere

Most veteran teachers will have had an experience similar to this one described by Michael Smith, a former high school English teacher who is currently a professor at Rutgers University.

> I used to torture my students with *The Scarlet Letter*. That's ironic because I loved the book. Every semester I taught it, I re-read it, and the book rewarded every re-reading. I'd come away with a more complete understanding of how well-crafted it was. And, of course, I wanted to share my insights with my students.

On about the tenth or eleventh reading, I discovered a hat motif (the "steeple-crowned" hats of the Puritan men, the contrast between the "skull-cap" of the Reverend John Wilson and the feather in Governor Bellingham's hat, and so on). Hard to believe I had missed it for so long. So among the lists my students were keeping in their notes was a list of hats.

I worked hard. I was enthusiastic. I wanted to give my students textual power by modeling what could be done in a close reading. I tried to engage them in the discussion of symbols and motifs that made *The Scarlet Letter* so rich for me. They hated it. They didn't care about hats. (Rabinowitz and Smith 1998, 103)

Thoughtful, caring teacher that he is, Michael Smith realized that his rereadings of *The Scarlet Letter* were actually making it harder for his students to make sense of the text. While he wanted to talk about hats, the students wanted to talk about why didn't Hester Prynne just leave if they treated her so badly. They wanted to know how on earth she could be interested in a wimp like Dimmesdale. And how ever could she have married that Chillingworth in the first place? By focusing on the aspects of the novel that only emerge after multiple readings, Smith—without meaning to—made his students feel incompetent.

I believe that we should reread a novel each time we teach it, but we must be on guard that all the things we know about a book from multiple rereadings don't create obstacles for students opening the text for the first time. I know I am guilty of showing off in front of the class from time to time, dazzling students with an explanation of some obscure mythological allusion, but I don't pretend that this is anything but my way of reminding them that I know a thing or two. I want them to know that it is in their best interest to pay attention. High school kids sometimes forget that there are a few things they can still learn from us.

When we take the symbolic hats approach to teaching a classic, what we forget is that most of the students in front of us don't plan to become English majors. Energetic teens have a lot more on their minds than literature. These kids are (mostly) willing to do what we ask as long as we don't go too far. My students love talking about big ideas but roll their eyes if I start to go on and on about the putrefaction motif in *Hamlet*. "You're getting symbol-minded, Mrs. Jago."

It makes good sense to let students know how a book is likely to challenge them as readers. Why let them think that there is something somehow wrong with them that is causing the book to be so difficult to read and the first chapter to seem so long? Why invite students to jump to the conclusion that *Frankenstein* is "Boring!" before they give the story a chance. When tackling a classic, students need to be prepared to adjust their recreational reading habits to a different kind of text. Which brings up another common obstacle to reading the classics: the belief that learning must be fun.

Does Learning Have to Be Fun?

One of the great fallacies about student achievement is that successful students love school. The real difference between successful and unsuccessful students has little to do with their proclivity for scholarly pursuits. The difference is in their willingness to do schoolwork.

What irks students is the work: paying attention, doing the reading, taking notes, studying for tests, writing papers. I don't blame them. But students who fail to discipline themselves to these onerous tasks learn very little. I wish it were otherwise. I wish that learning were as natural as breathing. It isn't. Reading a classic, like learning a language, takes applied effort.

Where educators have gone wrong is in promoting the idea that learning is fun. What follows from this faulty premise is the assumption that anything that isn't fun need not be completed. If the assignment feels like work, there must be something wrong with the book, or with the teacher, or maybe with the whole school. In fact learning can be enormous fun and with a good teacher often is, but fun is not the goal. The goal is learning.

No teacher with any sense would expect teenagers to love *Crime and Punishment* at first sight. A cursory glance at the 629-page novel sends the faint-hearted scurrying. For this reason, I always warn students that they are going to have to struggle a bit before they can enter Dostoevski's fictional world. I promise to be there to help and answer questions, but I explain that I can't do the work for them. If they want to know Raskolnikov, it is going to take effort. The "fun" comes later when students realize how much this extraordinary character has taught them about themselves.

Alerting Students to Textual Roadblocks

Reading complex literature poses challenges for all readers. Instead of pretending that obstacles don't exist, I address the potential stumbling blocks directly. Forewarned is forearmed.

Length

Yes, *Crime and Punishment* is a very long book. It is also a heavy book. Get over it. Trust me that I would never assign this novel if it weren't a glorious story and if I didn't love it myself. You are going to read things here that you will never forget. Some of the characters you meet on these pages are likely to live with you forever. (Ignore the smart aleck who tells you his house is already overcrowded.)

Vocabulary

You are likely to come across many unfamiliar words in this book. Try not to let this frustrate you. I'll help you learn how to make reasonable guesses about a word's meaning from context. We will also keep a list of the new words that we are learning. Developing your vocabulary is going to help you tremendously on the

SAT. (Reading a great book for the purpose of boosting one's SAT score seems a silly way to behave to me, but if it gets some students motivated, I'll use it; especially since I know they are going to get much, much more from the novel than some new vocabulary words.)

Syntax

Some sentences may at first seem hard to understand. They may be longer than the ones you are used to reading in newspapers and magazines. If you are a slow reader, you may find that by the time you get to the end of a sentence, you have forgotten what happened at the beginning. I will help you learn to pick up your pace. If the first pages really aren't making sense to you, you might try reading a few paragraphs out loud. This will help you hear the rhythm of the author's sentences. If you are embarrassed that someone in your family might hear you, take your book into the bathroom and turn on the shower.

Unfamiliar Settings and Time Periods

Every novel invites you to enter a fictional world. Finding your way in that world is always easiest when the fictional world has a lot in common with the world you know. The more foreign the world is to your own, the harder you may feel the book is to "get into." But don't give up. One of the greatest joys of reading is traveling to places you will never see. Who wants to know only the neighborhood where fate dropped you? Don't be put off by descriptions of landscapes that you can't quite picture. Ask questions! I'm sure others in the class are having the very same difficulty. You may also come across allusions to political figures or historical events that are unfamiliar. Sometimes these references are essential to the story's development, but often they are not. Put a Post-it note next to the allusion and ask about it in class. If I don't know the answer to your question, I will help you find it.

Unfamiliar Character Names

I always have trouble at the beginning of a novel when several characters' names begin with the same letter. What I have learned to do is make myself pronounce the names out loud. This seems to get them into my head more firmly. If you know that you struggle to keep characters straight, make an annotated list of character names on a Post-it note and keep this inside the front cover. Some novels include a family tree. You might think of creating one for yourself if you find yourself getting confused.

Format

Unless you have read many plays, the format of a drama can be very confusing. Start by reading the cast of characters and any introductory notes the playwright offers. If you skip this section, it will be harder to visualize the characters' actions on stage. Don't gloss over italicized explanations of how a line is to be delivered, either. Often your best clues to the content of a scene are to be found within parentheses. A good example of this can be found on the final page of act 1 of August Wilson's (1986) Pulitzer Prize–winning play *Fences*.

CORY: Mama!
ROSE: Troy. You're hurting me.
TROY: Don't you tell me about no taking and giving.

(*CORY comes up behind TROY and grabs him. TROY, surprised, is thrown off balance just as CORY throws a glancing blow that catches him on the chest and knocks him down. TROY is stunned, as is CORY.*)

ROSE: Troy. Troy. No!
(*TROY gets to his feet and starts at CORY.*)
Troy ... no. Please! Troy!
(*ROSE pulls on TROY to hold him back. TROY stops himself.*)

TROY: *(To CORY.)* Alright. That's strike two. You stay away from around me, boy. Don't you strike out. You living with a full count. Don't you strike out.

(TROY exits out the yard as the lights go down.)

While this scene may occupy only a very few minutes on the stage, it may take several readings before you can fully understand what is going on among these characters.

Helping Students Adjust Their Reading Rates

By describing the potential minefields, I hope to prevent student readers from getting blown to bits by a challenging text. I also hope to prepare them for shifting into a different kind of reading mode when they pick up a classic. English teachers are acutely aware of the difference between the way they read a story in *Cosmopolitan* or *Maxim* (guiltily and surreptitiously) while waiting in a grocery store line and the way they read a passage from Jane Austen. Many students see no such distinction. Reading is reading. Their eyes move across a line of print and down the page at much the same rate with much the same level of attention, whatever the text in their hands.

In order to help students become more aware of their rate of reading I have them figure out how fast they read. My methods here are quite unscientific and designed only to give students ballpark-range figures. I ask them to bring to class a book that they find easy to read, not a picture book or a magazine but something that interests them and that poses no textual challenges. I always have plenty of popular titles available for those who forget their book. With ninth-grade students, I find Francesca Lia Block's Weetzie Bat books or any of Chris Crutcher's novels work well. With eleventh and twelfth graders, I often hand them a Michael Crichton or Steven King book.

I then have students follow these steps:

1. Record their starting page number.
2. Read for twenty minutes without pausing.
3. Record their ending page number.
4. Determine how many pages they have read.
5. Multiply the number of pages by 3 to give them the number of pages they are able to read in an hour.

I remind students that differences in the number of words on a page make a big difference in the rate of their reading. What they have here is a rough estimate of how fast they move along when reading for pleasure.

I then ask students to open up their copies of *Frankenstein* (or whatever classic we are studying) and to repeat these steps. Invariably, students find that Mary Shelley's prose slows them down quite a bit. I tell them that this is a good thing—that unfamiliar vocabulary, complex syntax, and a complicated story all contribute to making this text a slower read than the books they peruse for recreation. I also suggest that in order to enjoy Shelley's gorgeous use of language better they might want to slow down even more.

I then ask students to calculate how long it will take them to complete the night's homework assignment. For many students this is an epiphany. They never imagined they could actually figure out how much time they need to set aside to read a particular number of pages. Finally, we calculate how many hours it will take them to read the whole book. Students like knowing exactly how much of their lives they are going to have to devote to a text.

What I am trying to do here is give students greater control over their reading. Knowledge is power. If a student knows it is going to take her forty-five minutes to read Chapter 17, she can be more strategic about planning her after-school hours. If she knows she has soccer practice until 7 P.M. and fifteen problems due in math, she can see that there won't be much time for talking on the phone tonight. Or maybe she won't see that at all, but at least I have helped this student determine realistically how long the English homework will take.

Often students enjoy figuring out approximately how many pages they can read in a minute. Fast readers typically cover close to a page a minute. Two minutes per page for a difficult book is about average, but when students require more than four minutes a page, I worry that they are getting so bogged down negotiating sentences that they lose the drift of the story.

Is Good-Enough Reading Good Enough?

In a fascinating piece of research titled "Good-Enough Reading: Momentum and Accuracy in the Reading of Complex Fiction," Margaret Mackey (1997) illustrates how readers engage in a good-enough reading, striking a personal balance between the need for momentum and the need for accountability to the text. She opens her article with this caveat:

> Reading is an event in time: complex, untidy, and inevitably partial. Often when reading researchers talk about reading they inadvertently or otherwise camouflage the inherent messiness of readers' temporal accommodations to a text by referring to post-reading responses. Such responses apply a retrospective coherence to a swarm of impressions and associations that can only gain any real shapeliness after the reading act itself is concluded. Much reading research and literary theorizing also magnifies the effect of coherence by dealing with short, highly crafted texts. (428)

What Mackey found as she examined the reading habits of middle school, high school, and university students was that readers vary in their tolerance for good-enough readings. Some favor momentum; others place a greater value on accuracy. But "no reader can entirely ignore the need for momentum; reading must ultimately move forward if it is to occur at all" (429). Instead of calling a halt to their reading while they investigate a detail, good readers create a temporary interpretation that enables them to keep reading.

> They develop provisional understandings: they simply take note that something is important and keep on reading without pausing to fret over its complete significance; they provide affective substitutes from their own personal experiences when they cannot immediately make a cultural reference; they carry on even when they are not clear that their understanding of the story is accurate or appropriate, hoping for clarity to develop over time. (455)

I wondered if learning how to do this kind of "good-enough" reading might help some of my slower readers. I urged students to proceed with less than complete information, to keep moving forward on the page even if they don't quite understand what is happening in the story. Obviously such a strategy can backfire and leave a reader confused and misled. But the more I thought about how I read, confidently assuming that anything that doesn't make sense now will all come clear in the end, the more convinced I became that encouraging students to move ahead with a partial understanding would ultimately help them stay engaged with the book.

In complex novels, the story line is seldom a clear path from Point A to Point B. The author may choose to begin in the middle, as in *The Odyssey*, or even toward the very end, and take the reader backwards in time with flashbacks or other storytelling devices. Sometimes the relationships among characters seem to make no sense. Other times, the fictional world is so foreign to the reader that simply exploring the terrain is a formidable challenge. Experienced readers learn to forge ahead, confident that the writer won't lead them astray. Have they missed or misunderstood some important information? Most likely. But the absence of these details doesn't block the reader's forward progress. Good-enough reading keeps students engaged and actively revising their understanding of the story as it unfolds.

I hasten to add that there are times when "good-enough" readings are most certainly not good enough. It would be a disaster to float along through three chapters of a biology or economics textbook assuming that confusing concepts will all come clear in the end. With informational texts, each piece of information is important to register and store. New vocabulary needs to be clearly defined on the spot rather than guessed at from context.

There are also times when "good-enough" reading is not good enough in a literature class either. Mackey explains:

> It is important to note that acknowledging the role of good-enough reading in the real-time experiences of readers is not the same as being satisfied with good-enough readings as the best that can be accomplished in a literature class. Good-enough reading will sometimes suffice for a particular individual on a private occasion, but teachers naturally hope and expect to move beyond that point in the collective readings that occur in the classroom. Nevertheless, it is important to be aware that much of the activity that occurs in readers' minds, beyond the reach of teacher or other co-readers, is contingent, incomplete, and messy, that this is actually part of how reading works. (457)

"Incomplete and messy" certainly describes what goes on in many of my students' minds as they negotiate a challenging text. What always surprises me, though, is how often their messy and incomplete readings startle me into new understandings of a book I thought I knew inside out.

Nobody Reads the Same Book Twice

Robertson Davies (1988), celebrated author of *What's Bred in the Bone, The Deptford Trilogy,* and many other celebrated novels, said in his *Tanner Lectures on Human Values* that

> The great sin is to assume that something that has been read once has been read forever. As a very simple example I mention Thackeray's *Vanity Fair.* People are expected to read it during their university years. It should be read again when you are 36, which is the age of Thackeray when he wrote it. It should be read for a third time when you are 56, 66, 76, in order to see how Thackeray's irony stands up to your own experience of life. Perhaps you will not read every page in these later years, but you really should take another look at a great book, in order to find out how great it is, or how great it has remained, to you. You see, Thackeray was an artist, and artists deserve this kind of careful observation. We must not gobble their work, like chocolates or olives, or anchovies, and think we know it forever. Nobody ever reads the same book twice. (87)

As a reader I have always tended to be a gobbler, devouring books and then checking off a mental list as "Read." But as Davies explains, great books invite rereadings. What this means for teachers is that we needn't worry when students only seem to be taking in a small portion of what a novel has to offer or when they miss the hats in *The Scarlet Letter.* We must trust that if we have done our job well, they will come back to these books later in life and the books themselves will teach them more.

CHAPTER THREE

Negotiating Story Structures

In 1838 Henry David Thoreau wrote in his journal (Dec. 31), "As the least drop of wine colors the whole goblet, so the least particle of truth colors our whole life. It is never isolated, or simply added as dollars to our stock. When any real progress is made, we unlearn and learn anew, what we thought we knew before." Every group of students I meet causes me to unlearn and learn anew. I keep hoping that one day I'll get it all figured out, but some new particle of truth always seems to be coloring the water.

A few things have remained constant. During these years I have been in the same classroom facing the same desks, gazing out over the heads of my students through the same dirty windows. On September 15th, I hand out copies of *The Odyssey*. Stop by in February, and you will find me reading *Julius Caesar*. But beneath these superficial constants, my teaching has shifted quite dramatically.

One drop of truth that caused me, in Thoreau's words, to "unlearn and learn anew" was the realization that for many children, simply rubbing up against books wasn't going to make them love literature. It began to dawn on me that if I wanted students to achieve the deep literacy I wrote about in Chapter 1, I was going to have to experiment with a dangerous practice, "direct instruction."

Like many other teachers in the early 1990s, I was an indefatigable optimist. I believed in a kind of literary field of dreams. Build the ideal classroom, and they will come. Offer them books, and they will read. While teachers elsewhere have made such classrooms work, I was having trouble ignoring the fact that many of my thirty-six ethnically diverse urban scholars were not growing as readers the way I hoped they would. In my own English department I saw teacher after teacher abandon *Great Expectations* and *Huckleberry Finn,* insisting that second-language learners simply didn't have the reading skills to comprehend these difficult texts. Honors students, of course, continued to be assigned both.

In her disturbing book, *Other People's Children,* Lisa Delpit (1995) raises the thorny issue of what happens to minority and underprivileged students when skills are devalued in the classroom:

> A critical thinker who lacks the skills demanded by employers and institutions of higher learning can aspire to financial and social status only within the disenfranchised underword. . . . If minority people are to effect the change which will allow them to truly progress we must insist on skills within the context of critical and creative thinking. (19)

Delpit suggests an alternative to child-centered and process methods for minority children. She explains:

> I do not advocate a simplistic "basic skills" approach for children outside of the culture of power. It would be (and has been) tragic to operate as if these children were incapable of critical and higher-order thinking and reasoning. Rather, I suggest that schools must provide these children the content that other families from a different cultural orientation provide at home. This does not mean separating children according to family background, but instead, ensuring that each classroom incorporate strategies appropriate for all the children in its confines. (30)

How a Story Works

Delpit got me thinking. Maybe the reason non-honors students didn't have the "reading skills" teachers deemed necessary for negotiating the classics was that we hadn't taught them very well. I am not speaking here about teaching students how to read but rather about teaching students how stories work. In our urgency to abandon the lecture format, literature teachers may have adopted too passive a role. Clearly we want to continue to make genuine student response the cornerstone of the classroom, but withholding information about how a story works may make it impossible for some students to have any response at all.

One has only to consider Toni Morrison's *Beloved* and *Jazz* or Salman Rushdie's *Midnight's Children* to see that truly "novel" texts continue to be written. But writers build stories with a common set of blocks, drawing from a stock of possibilities familiar to any experienced reader: A hero/heroine engages the reader's sympathy. A problem develops. A foil appears to allow the reader to see the hero/heroine more clearly. The problem gets worse. Help appears. More complications arise, but the hero/heroine prevails. All is resolved. Sometimes, in the words of the Prince at the conclusion of *Romeo and Juliet*, "All are punish'd."

While such story structures may be so familiar to an English teacher that they hardly bear commenting upon, this is not the case for many high school readers. Some of my students have touched only books that teachers put in their hands and have never, in fact, read a single one from cover to cover. One approach to solving this problem is to create a vibrant outside reading program within every English classroom. Another is to use the classics to teach students how stories work. I do not believe it is a matter of either/or. Students need both.

Let me use Mary Shelley's *Frankenstein, or the Modern Prometheus* as an example. Now I am quick to admit the weaknesses of the lecture format when used day after day with teenagers. But the

---

first pages of Shelley's novel pose inexperienced readers with a real problem. The story opens with a group of letters written by Robert Walton, an explorer adrift in the Arctic Sea, to his sister in London. Without a few words from me about the epistolary format and about how Walton becomes, like us, the listener to Victor Frankenstein's strange tale, many students are lost before they have even begun. The simplest of clues and guiding questions seem to help:

1. What do you notice about the dates of these letters?
2. Why do you think Robert writes to his sister if there is no way to post the letters?
3. What does Robert reveal about himself here?
4. Where does Mary Shelley (through Robert) explain to the reader how the format of her story will now change?
5. Can you think of any other stories or movies that are structured like this?

My questions aim to tease out from students an understanding of how Shelley's story is structured. I think it unrealistic to assume that most of them can be assigned these pages to read and that they will figure out the structure for themselves. Victor Frankenstein doesn't start telling the story students thought they were going to hear until page 30. If I don't offer some guidance—a kind of reader's map—through the first 29, too many give up.

It also doesn't seem fair to teach novels like *Frankenstein* only to students who instinctively understand how a series of one-sided letters like Robert Walton's works. When my colleagues in the English department urge that we simplify the curriculum for struggling students and replace the classics with shorter, more accessible novels, I know they are motivated by kindness. But the real kindness would be to give all students the tools to handle challenging texts. We aren't being paid simply to assist students who hardly need us. We're being paid to find a way for all students to develop as readers.

So I tell my students about how stories work. I remind them to pay close attention to who is narrating the story and to whom. Where appropriate, I point out foreshadowing. I don't monopolize the classroom conversations, but I don't hold back either when I feel that students are lost.

Connections Beyond the Story

Students had read about half of *Frankenstein*, but they were restless. I can always tell when their reading of a piece of literature is losing momentum by the snippets of conversation floating up to my desk. "Nothing happens." "I fell asleep and missed the part where the monster came to life." "Victor Frankenstein just rambles." And most ominous of all, "Boring."

I love this book and thought I had been doing a pretty good job of teaching the Gothic tale of pride and prejudice (my own interpretation, which I love talking about to anyone who will listen), but something was missing. The students weren't hooked. I knew they were doing the reading because our discussion the day before about Victor Frankenstein's passion for his research had gone very well. Their eyes were dutifully passing over the pages, but their hearts just weren't in it.

The lesson I had planned was going to be a close look at Mary Shelley's use of language, examining how syntax and diction created the story's tone. But experience told me that I had better think fast if I didn't want to spend the hour asking questions nobody except me cared much about. Rummaging through my *Frankenstein* files, I found a magazine article about cloning that raised the question, "Are there some scientific experiments that should never be conducted?" Handing out copies of this essay to the class, I asked students what they thought. Are there some scientific advances that the human race is not and never will be able to handle?

Hands flew into the air. Students saw at once the connection between the moral dilemma of cloning and Victor Frankenstein's creation. They argued that even the obvious medical advantage of being able to clone new hearts or livers would soon be outweighed by the cloning of super-soldiers. The science fiction buffs in the room had a field day telling tales of genetically engineered races destroying the world. Many students had recently read *Brave New World* and used Aldous Huxley's dystopia as an example of what can happen when scientists rather than humanists run the show.

My role as teacher shifted from Grand Inquisitor to traffic controller. "First Allen, then Melinda, then Andrew. We'll get to you, Joe. Hold on." The hardest part was making sure students were listening to one another rather than simply waiting their turn to expound. I complimented those who began their comments with a reference to something someone else had said. This helped. When the conversation turned to the question of whether science might someday make religion obsolete, I thought the windows might explode from the passionate intensity of their arguments. They had so much to say.

At the bell, the room erupted into a dozen conversations. A handful of students bolted to the bookshelf where I had copies of *Brave New World*. I shouted over the din that they needed to read Chapters 12 through 14 of *Frankenstein* by Monday. Spent, I collapsed at my desk, reasonably certain that the big ideas in Mary Shelley's novel had finally come alive for these readers. The rest of *Frankenstein* should make better sense now. And to think that some people consider teaching literature genteel, scholarly work.

I resolved that tomorrow we would review our rules of classroom discussion:

- Students must talk to one another, not just to me or to the air.

- Students must listen to one another. To ensure that this happens, they must either address the previous speaker or offer a reason for changing the subject.

- Students must all be prepared to participate. If I call on someone and he or she has nothing to say, the appropriate response is, "I'm not sure what I think about that, but please come back to me."

Yvonne Hutchison, master teacher at one of the most challenging middle schools in the Los Angles Unified School District, helped me create this set of coherent guidelines for classroom discussion. She asserts that we must assume that all students have important things to say but that many of them are unfamiliar with the rules of scholarly discourse. A few students seem to know these rules instinctively. But if we want all students to participate in civil classroom discussion, we need to teach them how.

Student-run Discussions and Projects

One method that has worked for me has been to put student desks into a circle and call the day's lesson a "seminar." The word itself seems to lend an air of importance to the discussion. I then do the following:

1. Tell students that everyone must participate at least once during the seminar.

2. Explain to students that no one needs to raise a hand to be called on, but all students should be sensitive to each other, noticing when someone seems to have something to say but may be too shy to jump into the conversation. I give them the words they might use: "Luke, you look as though you disagree. What are you thinking?" If a quiet student can't

be heard, I tell other students that they must ask him or her to speak up. This shows they really want to know what this person has to say.

3. Teach students how to deal with the compulsive talkers in their midst. Pointing out how even motor-mouthed Diana must at some point inhale, I tell them that this is the moment when others can politely interrupt. (I say this lovingly, and the Dianas in the class always laugh. They know that others stop listening when they rattle on for too long.)

4. Tell students that silence is a part of the seminar, too. It means people are thinking. If the silence goes on for too long, they might want to open up *Frankenstein* and see if there is a particular passage they would like to ask one another about. They might want to read the passage aloud.

5. Let students know that I will be sitting outside their circle and that I must remain silent until the last five minutes of class. I will be taking notes of things I observe occurring during the seminar and will be sharing these with them. My comments will not be about the content of their discussion but rather about how students have conducted themselves. I focus on the positive behaviors, the subtle ways in which students help one another join in the discussion.

In my experience such seminars work best with twenty or fewer students. With my larger classes I have tried dividing the students into two groups, but it never seems to work quite as well. My presence—my silent, note-taking self, sitting outside the circle—is a key piece of what makes students take the seminar seriously. I have yet to figure out how to clone myself so I can watch two groups at once.

Last fall after students had finished reading both *Beowulf* and John Gardner's *Grendel* (the Beowulf story told from the point of view of the monster), I told students that instead of taking a test or writing a comparison/contrast essay about the two books, we would hold a seminar. Since this was to take the place of a formal assessment, everyone would have to speak up and participate. Students readily agreed. As I wasn't going to be asking the questions or calling upon them, it was up to the group to generate the discussion and, in so doing, to demonstrate to me their understanding of the two books.

Melinda began: "The last line in *Grendel* made me think again about how I felt about the monster. I mean the whole book sets you up to sympathize with him, but look how he finishes: 'Poor Grendel's had an accident. *So may you all.*' That's really mean and malicious."

"I agree. It's blood-lust." remarked Joe. "This is an evil monster who deserved to be killed." But Nicole saw it differently. "Wait, look at how he was treated in his life, no mother he could talk to, Beowulf out to get him, no friends, no one to teach him how to behave."

Jorge interrupted, "Grendel was just something in the hero's way, something for the hero to slay so he could win fame and have lots of people sing about him."

"That's how it was in *Beowulf*," Nicole continued, "but in Gardner's book you could see how the monster felt. You knew what he was thinking. In a way, I think Grendel was trapped in a role. I feel sorry for him."

The conversation continued in this vein for the next forty minutes. To anyone who delights in watching teenagers learn, the interval was breathtaking. Students listened to one another, probed each other's observations, pointed to the text. When it was over I could have hugged every one of them. Instead, I let them know that this was as good as the study of literature gets. All the other activities and exercises we complete along the way are simply preparation for this kind of exchange, for just this kind of conversation among readers about texts.

———

After class Melinda came up to let me know that they really should have had more time for the discussion. I often wonder if students are as blunt with all their teachers. No one ever seems to hesitate to tell me what I should do better. Of course, she was right.

I remember another group of students who had finished reading *Frankenstein*. It was the year when trials were all the rage in Los Angeles: the Menendez brothers, Heidi Fleiss, O. J. Simpson. My students were experts on courtroom drama and procedures. Sophomore Mike Regalbuto had the idea that we should put Victor Frankenstein on trial for the murders his monster committed. The class loved the idea. Within a few days roles were assigned, teams of attorneys had been to the library for research, robes were found for the judge, and court was in session. Students had the protocols down pat.

My favorite moment occurred when the defense put Dr. Alfred Nobel on the stand. Rebecca Rainoff asked the eminent scientist if he felt he should be held responsible for the destructive uses dynamite has been put to in the world. He said, "Of course not." To which Rebecca responded, "If Dr. Nobel is not culpable for the destruction his creation, dynamite, has wrought, then how can you, the jury, convict Victor Frankenstein for what his creation has done? I rest my case."

Scaffolding for Diction and Syntax

These students were caught up in the lesson. I can't remember anyone asking me for a grade on the project. The quality of their production was recompense enough. They saw their work and knew it was good. But I don't believe most of these students would have been able to move beyond the text with such confidence without considerable instructional scaffolding along the way. Young readers are unused to negotiating sentences like this:

I was hurried away by fury; revenge alone endowed me with strength and composure; it mounded my feelings and allowed me to be calculating and calm at periods when otherwise delirium or death would have been my portion. (Shelley 1994, 192)

The help students needed was simple enough to provide: "See all those semicolons? For a minute pretend they are periods. Does the passage make sense to you now? Why do you think Shelley chose to string those ideas together? What effect does the longer sentence have on you as a reader? How is this different from the effect created by a series of shorter ones?" I drew students' attention to the way in which punctuation is often a guide to negotiating complex syntax. We needed to unpack only a few sentences like this together before students found that they could manage Shelley's syntax on their own.

Diction was another challenge. Borrowing the idea and the butcher paper from a first-grade teacher, I posted a word wall. As we read through the novel, students posted words they found whose meaning they did not know. As I wanted to make this a lesson in building meaning from context clues, I asked students to indicate where in the text the word could be found. From a single night's reading they collected the following:

sullen

epoch

precipices

pallid

immutable

pinnacle

mutability

dissipated

odious

dormant

slaked

cabriolet

prognosticate

depravity

ignominious

wantonly

timorous

approbation

guile

obdurate

perdition

inexorable

My goal was to encourage students to explore the range of Mary Shelley's vocabulary. They shared the words they found and tried to figure out what each word meant based on how it was used in the sentence as well as on what they knew about what was going on in the story at that moment. Quite often their guesses were on target. We turned to the *Oxford English Dictionary* only to verify our estimations. Doing this kind of word study together teaches students strategies for negotiating a passage full of unfamiliar words. Making connections between unfamiliar words and familiar words—for example *mutability* with *mutant* and *prognosticate* with *prognosis*—also demonstrates to students that they know more than they think they know. It helps build their confidence as readers of difficult prose.

I also hoped that students would begin to see how the more words an author has at her disposal, the more subtle her prose can be. Was I teaching "basic skills"? I suppose so, but it never felt as though I had distorted Shelley's text as I did so.

Teaching Students About Reading Theory

Another method for working with challenging texts is to teach students about theories of reading. Most students have no idea that reading is a much-studied act and that entire schools of thought have grown out of this primary skill. Few students have ever given much thought to their own reading beyond "I like to read" or "I don't like to read." In *You Gotta BE the Book,* Jeff Wilhelm (1997) describes research that he conducted in his middle school classroom examining the habits of teenage readers. I cannot do justice here to the complexity of Wilhelm's research, but his case studies of three engaged readers point the way to classroom instruction that can help all students become accomplished readers. Wilhelm found that

> the response of engaged readers is intensely visual, empathic, and emotional. By focusing in class on the importance of these evocative responses, that is, entering the story world, visualizing people and places, and taking up relationships to characters, less engaged readers were given strategies for experiencing texts and were helped to rethink reading. (144)

Wilhelm challenges teachers to consider:

> *Why do some kids love reading? What is rewarding and engaging about reading for these students? What do these engaged readers "do" as they read that makes the experience fun, satisfying, and engaging for them?*
>
> *Why do other kids hate reading? What in their experience has contributed to their negative view?*
>
> I realized that year after year, I had encountered students who obviously resisted reading. But they seemed to be a minority, and eventually—I'm ashamed to say—I'd really just given up on them

as far as becoming readers was concerned. It was when I encountered a whole class of them that I could not blame them instead of myself, the materials, or the method. Eighth grade remedial reading produced a crisis that required a new way of thinking about and teaching the act of reading. If I wished to pursue my job of developing readers, then resistance and lack of engagement were compelling issues that had to be deeply considered. (7)

Pursuing answers to these questions, Wilhelm experimented with incorporating discussions about reading theory and literary conventions into his lessons. What he found was that as students became increasingly aware of the fact that they were actually going to have to "do" something to make a text comprehensible, their frustrations with reading decreased. Suddenly it wasn't that anything was wrong with them (or with the text) causing them to find a book incomprehensible, but that they simply weren't doing the things that good readers do when they read. As Umberto Eco (1994) explains, "Every text is a lazy machine asking the reader to do some of its work."

Without diminishing the importance of good early reading instruction or the difficulties children with disabilities face when reading, I would like to assert that many "poor readers" are actually lazy readers. This is not a reflection on their character. It's simply that no one ever told these children that reading was going to be work. Even when students dutifully eyeball the assigned pages, few think the homework assignment has asked them for anything more. Students turn on their stereos, kick back on their beds, and expect the book to transfer information from its pages to their brains. While such a passive stance might work perfectly well for reading *Surfer* magazine, it is grossly inadequate for texts like *The Odyssey*.

An exchange between two of Wilhelm's students—one an engaged reader, the other a struggling reader—demonstrates how broad the chasm is between students who don't and do know what a text demands of a reader:

John: I can't believe you do all that stuff when you read! Holy crap,
I'm not doing . . . like nothing . . . compared to you.

Ron: I can't believe you don't do something. If you don't, you're not
reading, man. . . . It's gotta be like wrestling or watching a movie or
playing a video game . . . you've got to like . . . be there! (xiii)

Reading as a Creative Act

I want students to know that it is not enough simply to eyeball a
page of print and expect the story to come alive or even make sense.
A reader needs to act. Louise Rosenblatt (1983) explains:

> The benefits of literature can emerge only from creative activ-
> ity on the part of the reader himself. He responds to the little
> black marks on the page, or to the sounds of the words in his
> head, and he "makes something of them." The verbal symbols
> enable him to draw on his past experiences with what the words
> point to in life and literature. The text presents these words in
> a new and unique pattern. Out of these he is enabled actually
> to mold a new experience, the literary work. (278)

The challenge for any literature teacher is to make these "creative activities" visible to students. Struggling readers often have no
idea about the things that expert readers do inside their heads when
they read. According to Rosenblatt, good readers conduct a trans-
action with the text. The reader creates meaning from the words on
the page while the text causes the reader to reexamine what he or
she knows. The text and the reader interact.

What is so powerful to me about Rosenblatt's work is how she
situates the study of literature at the center of every child's life. It is
not only the college-bound or future English teachers who need the
nourishment that literature can provide, but all students. She explains that "literature makes comprehensible the myriad ways in

which human beings meet the infinite possibilities that life offers" (6). For most students, for most readers of any age, what is most important is the human experience that literature presents. "The reader seeks to participate in another's vision—to reap knowledge of the world, to fathom the resources of the human spirit, to gain insights that will make his own life more comprehensible" (7).

Last year I taught a class of extremely reluctant ninth-grade readers. In this small class of twenty, there were seven special education students and five ESL students. The four girls in the class staked out their territory in the desks near the door. As I handed out copies of *Romeo and Juliet,* I told the class that this story was going to remind them a lot of people they know and situations they've experienced. We worked our way through the play—acting out scenes, discussing the characters, drawing parallels to teenage life as they knew it. In their journals, students wrote about arguments they had had with their parents and fights they had witnessed. We studied the formal elements of Shakespeare's play, but only as they functioned in terms of the total literary experience. Feeling and connection had to come first.

Rosenblatt theorizes that literature is a form of personal experience and that as such it "has many potentialities that dynamic and informed teaching may sustain" (222). I interpret her discoveries as follows:

1. Literature fosters the imagination that any healthy democracy needs—the ability to understand the needs and hopes of others and the ability to see how our actions affect other people's lives.

2. Literature offers readers images of behavior and attitudes other than their own.

3. Literature teaches teenagers about the many possible ways of life, including a variety of philosophies from which the reader is then free to choose.

4. Literature can help readers make sound choices through vicarious trial and error or experimentation—through experiencing in the text the consequences of characters' actions.

5. Literature can assist readers to view their own personalities and problems objectively and so to handle them better.

6. Literature, through which teenagers meet a wide range of temperaments and value systems, may free them from fears, guilt, and insecurity engendered by too narrow a view of normality.

7. Literature can offer socially beneficial avenues for impulses that might otherwise find expression in antisocial behavior.

Many of the students in my ninth-grade class were adept at antisocial behavior. Getting them to sit still for more than ten minutes and to participate in classroom discussion without putting one another down was a daily challenge. But as we made our way through *Romeo and Juliet*, I felt that what Rosenblatt describes was occurring before my eyes. These students' behavior was a result of their insecurity. As we talked and wrote about how the Montagues and Capulets as well as gangs on our campus behaved toward one another, students seemed to expand their sense of normalcy. Carlos, a bilingual student who has attended several different schools both in Los Angeles and in Puerto Rico over the course of his fourteen years, compared the Prince's final speech with our school principal's rule that anyone involved in a fight will automatically be expelled. Here is the speech:

Capulet, Montague,
See what a scourge is laid upon your hate,
That heaven finds means to kill your joys with love!
And I, for winking at your discords too,
Have lost a brace of kinsmen. All are punish'd.
(*Romeo and Juliet*, act 5, scene 3)

And here is our dialogue:

Carlos: I don't think the principal's rule is fair because if someone disrespects me I'm not going to let it go, but I guess she doesn't want to be caught winking at our fights.

Me: Why do you think that is?

Carlos: Oh, she probably feels responsible when anybody on campus gets hurt, which I don't agree with either but I think that's just the way she is.

Diana [the most excitable and outspoken of the four girls in the class, also bilingual]: You know Lettie who was in this class the first week? She got kicked out for fighting and sent to Uni (University High School). The principal didn't care who started it. She just expelled everybody.

Carlos: I think she wanted to make an example for other kids. If the principal says "community" one more time, I think I'm gonna hit somebody.

Me: Don't, Carlos. You know it would break her heart to lose a brace of students.

The Importance of Close Reading

Careless interpretations of Rosenblatt's theory of reader response have led some teachers to abandon the practice of close reading. What is unfortunate about this loss is that student responses, however heartfelt, which are based upon casual or inaccurate readings are often inaccurate and lead the reader into confusion rather than to understanding. Teachers need to take time in class to show students how to examine a text in minute detail: word by word, sentence by sentence. Anne E. Berthoff (1999) claims that the chief means of teaching critical reading and writing is to "offer students assisted invitations to look and look again at words, sentences, paragraphs" (676). Only then will they develop the skills they need to be powerful readers. Berthoff goes on to explain:

> The disappearance of close reading is not to be confronted with the calm resignation (or secret jubilation?) evinced by those redrawing the boundaries. Without it, as the chief instrument of Practical Criticism, "reader response" is merely personal, merely psychological, merely opinion. The chief value of Practical Criticism is that it is—practical: it is pragmatic. Close reading teaches that the transactions with the text are always tentative and subject to the pragmatic maxim: "If we take it—metaphor, syntax, word, line—this way, what difference would it make to the way we read the rest of the poem? The opus? The age?" Close reading is entailed in critical reading. It is not an elitist, nose-to-the text, words-on-the-page pedantry but the way of attending to the interplay of saying and meaning. (677)

The kind of close reading that Berthoff describes does not come naturally to teenagers. When explaining what they think about what they have read, most prefer a broad brushstroke rather than a fine line of reasoning. The challenge for the teacher is to help students refine how they examine a piece of literature without destroying their confidence as readers. I start with students' responses but then ask prodding questions that encourage students to return to the text for answers:

- You say you hate the way Odysseus lies to everyone he meets when he returns to Ithaca. Let's look at that scene with Penelope again. What is Odysseus trying to find out with his lies?

- The scene where Odysseus's dog dies of a broken heart upon seeing his master is one of my favorite scenes, too. What does this moment tell you about Odysseus? Read those lines again. What does the state the dog is in tell you about the state of Odysseus's kingdom?

- It is indeed "gross" when all the unfaithful serving maids are hanged. Look at the epic simile Homer uses to describes this scene: "As when either thrushes with their long wings or doves / Rush into a net that has been set in a thicket, / As they come in to roost, and a dreadful bed takes them in; / So they held their heads in a row, and about the necks / Of all there were nooses, that they might die most piteously. / They struggled a little with their feet, but not very long" [309]. Why do you think Homer compares the serving women to birds?

Teachers need to go beyond encouraging responses from student readers and push them to understand exactly what the author has done with words and sentences, syntax, and diction that elicited such a response in them as readers.

Berthoff concludes her essay, which is called "Reclaiming the Active Mind":

> I have been suggesting that close reading and close observation soften and sharpen hard, dull wits (and bright, confident wits) because they offer occasions to enjoy a pleasure in the exercise of the mind. To practice Practical Criticism by rehabilitating looking and looking again and reading slowly—and again—would thus be to reclaim the Imagination, the agency of the active mind. (680)

When the bell rings, I want students to leave class tired, exhausted from how well they have exercised their minds, yet happy about all they have accomplished.

As I reflect upon my own metamorphosis from nonjudgmental facilitator to a more assertive readers' guide, I think that what prompted my changes as much as Lisa Delpit's research was the realization that most student readers are nothing like me. When I was growing up I did little else but read. It wasn't a matter of having an unhappy childhood; I simply preferred characters in books for playmates. I read indiscriminately, helter-skelter, with no thought for improving my mind. I believed everyone and everything around me boring. Everything except for books.

I remember a Christmas day when I was fifteen. Trying to please a most difficult teenager, my godmother had given me a copy of Erich Segal's *Love Story*. I devoured the short novel in the interval between washing dishes and sit-around-the-tree-and-talk-about-old-times. I hated it. And loved hating it. Arrogantly scornful, I remember descending the stairs full of myself and certain that the sentimentality of Segal's story demonstrated beyond a shadow of a doubt the patent intellectual inferiority of my entire family.

I hasten to say that I have come to revise this point of view regarding my wonderful and most loving, indulgent family. I have penance done and like Samuel Taylor Coleridge's Ancient Mariner "penance more will do." But at fifteen I defined myself against this book chosen by someone who thought she knew me.

When my teachers began assigning classics like *A Tale of Two Cities, The Grapes of Wrath,* and *The Once and Future King,* I was in heaven. I loved the fact that the books were long and that these authors had lots of other books I could read next. I suppose if I had had more friends I might have discovered much earlier that most other teenagers didn't share my enthusiasms, but as it was I continued for years with my nose in a book.

When I became a teacher I quickly realized that most students are unwilling to do the amount of reading that I had taken for granted. I adjusted. But what took me much longer to figure out was just how much help students needed in order to be able to negotiate classic texts. I had come to these books with considerable reading experience. I didn't know how much I knew and had no names to put to the things I knew, but in a very deep way I understood how stories worked.

The students I teach, for the most part, have no such background. They have enormous experience and vast knowledge about a range of things that I was totally ignorant about at their age, of course, and about many aspects of life I continue to find baffling. I also assure you that every year I teach at least a half dozen avid, addicted readers. But apart from making sure that these students always have a book to read, they are not the ones who most need my help and expertise.

M. E. Kerr wrote a novel engagingly titled *I'll Love You When You're More Like Me*. Without meaning to, teachers often convey a similar message to students: "We'll teach you when you're more like us." Most teenagers will read exactly as much as is demanded of them. My own sixteen-year-old son would think nothing of stopping on page 43 if that was where the homework assignment ended—not even if he knew that the mystery was solved, the gun went off, the girl was saved on page 44. Discouraging? Yes. But as a teacher I need to learn to work with this.

Having a more realistic sense of my students' attitudes toward reading and their need for scaffolding when reading challenging texts has made me a better teacher. Does this make me a weakling for changing my mind about my methods? Not if, according to Thoreau, the "least particle of truth" can color our whole life. As long as I am a teacher, I intend to keep unlearning and learning anew what I thought before. It's my professional responsibility. It's also my passion.

CHAPTER FOUR

Rethinking What We Ask Students to Do

One of the most challenging aspects of assigning a classic is getting students to do the reading. Though some classics are short (see my list in Chapter 10), most novels by Austen, Dickens, Twain, Steinbeck, the Brontës, Dostoevsky, Tolstoy, Cather, Wharton, and Dreiser are more than three hundred pages long, a length almost inconceivable to many teenagers. What? Me read that?

Teachers brave enough to assign long novels often resort to one of two methods for holding students accountable. They punish and/or they reward. While it is easy to see how draconian punishments turn students off to reading, rewards can be just as dangerous. Browsing through the journal of the International Reading Association, I was startled to discover a news item praising an innovative program that paid students for reading books. Have educators lost their minds? Attaching a monetary reward to reading sends kids the message that reading is a painful task, worth doing only if they are otherwise compensated. Even worse is the Pizza Hut plan in which students earn free pizzas for completing a certain number of books. The sponsors of the program, people in the business of selling junk food and soft drinks, are doing their best to support education. It is not their fault that the underlying assumption—that children won't read without rewards—is wrong-headed.

Whenever we say, "If you do this, I'll give you that," we devalue *this*. Admittedly every parent alive has resorted to such bribery to cajole children into brushing teeth, putting on socks, and sleeping in their own beds. But by offering the reward of treats for what is simply reasonable behavior, we undermine the satisfaction inherent in completing these tasks for their own sake: healthy teeth, warm feet, rested parents. The same principle holds true for reading classical literature. By offering extrinsic incentives for completing a challenging novel, we inadvertently send students the message that no one would read this book simply for pleasure.

Rewards may increase the probability that children will accomplish something they don't particularly want to do, but the danger is that the reward ultimately changes the way they do it. Students lose sight of the real reward, what a great piece of literature has to offer them, and instead focus on the number of points needed to earn their pizza.

Sticks and Carrots

I had been intrigued by Alfie Kohn's (1993) book *Punished by Rewards,* but wanted to know more about what he thought about student motivation. So I called him up. The following conversation was published with Kohn's permission in *California English* (1995).

Carol Jago: Alfie, you've written that teachers should stop fiddling with grading systems and get on with the business of helping kids. As a teacher who has spent a lot of time devising point systems, I'm intrigued.

Alfie Kohn: Research into grading over recent years yields three conclusions: (i) that it induces less creative thinking, (ii) that it generates less interest in challenging tasks and texts, and (iii) that it diminishes students' interest in learning *per se*.

CJ: Pretty damning conclusions.

AK: Indeed. The only positive effect of grades tends to be a short-term recall of isolated facts and even that does not hold true for everyone.

CJ: Yet there is the counter-argument that without high-stakes grades for a final exam, students tend not to do the reading.

AK: Possibly, but that is a powerful indictment of what the grading system has done to kids' motivation until now, and possibly raises questions about curriculum. Research shows that when the curriculum is engaging and meaningful to students, there is no need to treat them as pets, to reward them with an A for doing what they are told with books they otherwise would not want to touch. Obviously it's much easier to resort to grades, as I must confess I used to do. It's more challenging, it takes more courage and skill, to take notice of students' lack of interest and take up the challenge to rethink what we are asking them to do.

CJ: Rhetoric in the current political climate suggests that if we would just teach what used to be taught in school everything will be fine.

AK: Yes. The traditional approach that secondary teachers have absorbed is the transmission view of education—cram them full of facts and skills that they can spit up on demand. This is inconsistent with the theory and research about how people learn. Many teachers are familiar with the idea of constructivism that says people of all ages are active meaning-makers, creating theories about themselves, the world, and the books they read, and that it is the teacher's job to facilitate that encounter. If you take that seriously, out go the multiple-choice tests along with the grades necessary to enforce them because they grow out of an antiquated set of assumptions about learning. There is a role for assessment: at some point we need to check in with students to get a sense of how well they're doing, how we can help them to learn more effectively next week. But before we look at assessment, we need to ask the more important question—why we want to assess students' work. If we're doing it to "motivate" them, there is a huge collection of evidence showing that this will be ineffective and counterproductive. When you reward people for doing something, as with an A, they tend to become less interested in what they were rewarded for doing. There is a huge amount of research that demonstrates the more you get students to focus on *how* they're doing, the less they're interested in *what* they're doing.

CJ: You have suggested that, in designing curriculum, teachers should apply a ten-year rule. What do you mean?

AK: Before a teacher, especially a middle-school or high-school instructor, sits down to plan a course, he or she should ask the question "What can I reasonably expect that students will retain from this course after a decade?" I know that if I'd been asked that question when I was teaching in high school and college, I would have found it profoundly unsettling, because I knew well, or would have known if I had been brave enough to face the question head-on, that all they would have left was a fact here, a stray theory there, a disconnected assumption or passage from a book. That should lead us to ask what it is we're doing.

CJ: What do you say to people who think that without grades students won't work as hard?

AK: To some extent that's true. It's an indictment of what grades have done to motivation, and it may be an indication of what's going on in that classroom. The last thing we want to do to a student whose interest and curiosity have been eroded by a stick and carrot approach is to offer more sticks and carrots. Better to challenge the myth that there is a single entity called "motivation" that kids can have more or less of. The truth is that there are different kinds of motivation and they are not equal, not equivalent. I always ask groups of teachers I address how many of them understand the difference between extrinsic and intrinsic motivation. Almost every hand goes up, but this doesn't transfer itself to the classroom. It's not just that intrinsic motivation is better; it's undermined by the use of extrinsic motivators. The problem is that it takes more effort to tap intrinsic interest than to say, "Listen up, folks, this is going to be on the test."

Holding Students Accountable for Their Reading

I came away from this conversation both encouraged and depressed. While I agree theoretically with everything Kohn says, my daily contact with real, live teenagers makes me absolutely certain that students need to be held accountable for their reading. The compromise I have struck has been to abandon quizzes that ask for simple recall of relatively unimportant detail (e.g., "Where did Raskolnikov hide the little boxes and jewelry he stole from the pawnbroker?"). Instead I select a key sentence or two from toward the end of the chapter that has been assigned and ask students to write for five minutes, placing this sentence within the context of the story. In the case of Part 2, Chapter 2 in *Crime and Punishment*, I gave a class of twelfth-grade students the following five-minute assignment:

> Explain the following quote from last night's homework. What is Raskolnikov talking about? What is bothering him?
>
> "Again an intense, almost unbearable joy overwhelmed him for an instant, as it had in the police office. 'I have buried my tracks!'"

Gauri Goyal, an intense and hard-working senior, responded:

> Raskolnikov just put the things he stole from the pawnbroker under a rock. He is acting crazy because the horror of crime he committed is starting to dawn on him though he can't admit this to himself. For a smart guy he seems kind of stupid to me. I mean

anyone could have seen him bury that stuff. I don't think he is thinking straight.

Rather than putting students on the spot to remember details, I ask them to reflect on how the novel is developing. If I choose the sentence carefully, students can't do this without having read the chapter. These short responses are also easy to read and evaluate—no small thing when you meet 150 students a day. I don't assign grades to the responses but simply give students credit or no credit for having done their homework.

Another day I checked up on students' reading by asking them to close their eyes and visualize the most powerful image they remembered from last night's reading. I then gave each one a large piece of white paper, told them to fold it to form four squares, and handed out boxes of crayons. In the top left corner I asked students to draw a picture of a powerful image from what they had read. Artistic talent was not required here, only a sincere effort at getting something of what was in their mind's eye on paper. In a second box I asked students to put this picture into words. Marty Schultz-Akerson wrote:

> Raskolnikov is catching the man who was following him and asks why he is doing so. The man looks Raskolnikov in the face and calls him a murderer. Raskolnikov freezes at the thought that someone knows he killed the two women. He doesn't understand how the man could know and racks his brain thinking about it. He goes back to his room and drifts into sleep. He has a dream that he goes to the pawnbroker's home and she is in the corner laughing. He tries to kill her but at every blow the laughter gets louder and louder.

In the third box I asked students to imagine they were professors of Russian Literature lecturing to a college class on the scene they just described from last night's reading. What I was hoping to elicit here was a shift from recounting of events to analysis. It was fascinating to note how students' syntax and diction shifted. In this box Marty wrote:

My dear students,

In this scene Raskolnikov is sent into a world of utter despair. A strange man has just called him a murderer. Raskolnikov knew he had outwitted the suspicious police officers, but suddenly here was a man calling him a murderer to his face. Where has this man come from? From inside Raskolnikov. The stranger tells Raskolnikov what he is—a murderer.

In the fourth box I invited students to write a poem, create a word collage, follow a stream of consciousness, or in any other way that suited them respond to the scene they had drawn. Lauren Santiago had been working with the meeting between Razumihin and Raskolnikov where Razumihin realizes what his friend has done. She created in a matter of seven or eight minutes the following found poem (to create a found poem, students choose luminous words and phrases from a prose text and rearrange them in the shape of a poem):

It was dark
They were looking at one another
In silence
Burning and intense eyes
Piercing into his soul
Into his consciousness
Something strange
Some idea, some hint
Slipped
Awful, hideous
"Do you understand now?"

This activity took up most of a class period but accomplished several instructional goals. I had a clear picture of which students had and had not completed the previous night's reading assignment. Students explored a scene from the novel that they—rather than the teacher—found powerful. They examined this moment from various perspectives. By prompting students to move quickly from one box to the next I hoped to keep them from feeling that they were creating a finished product. I was concerned with exercising their readers' minds. The resulting papers were not things of beauty to post on a bulletin board, but they were rich in ideas.

What kinds of grades did I assign to these papers? None. I had the information I needed regarding which students had done the homework, and students knew that I knew. In order that those who hadn't kept up with the reading wouldn't have to sit through the class period doing nothing, I asked these students to complete the identical steps for an earlier scene from the novel. The day's lesson was still valuable for them, but they knew they had been found out. Despite Alfie Kohn's warnings about internal versus external motivation, I still think teenagers keep up with their schoolwork better when they know their teacher cares enough to check up on them. No matter how tough they talk, my students feel bad when they let me down. Of course, I always give them another chance to make it up.

Quality Versus Quantity

A point of Kohn's that particularly resonated for me was his ten-year rule. I know exactly what I want my students to retain ten years hence: a love for the things that literature can do to them. It's not details from the books that I care about students being able to recall but the experience of having been moved by a book. While I believe that wide reading is a defining characteristic of a fully developed human being, I don't think this is determined by the number of books one has read. What matters more is the extent to which the books that have been read become integrated into students' lives.

My ten-year rule does not only hold for college-bound students whose linguistic backgrounds make a long-term relationship with literature seem, if not the most natural thing in the world, at least a reasonable goal. I intend that my struggling readers, my second-language learners, my truculent and reluctant scholars should also be moved by books. Making this happen is without doubt the most challenging task I face professionally. It's also the most important one.

Keeping a Record of Students' Reading

Many teachers in the English department at Santa Monica High School have students keep a log of all the books they read in the course of the year. These are kept in students' portfolios, and when the folders move from one grade to the next, students can continue their list. I like this addition to a writing portfolio because it offers evidence of a student's reading history. The document also allows for interesting senior reflection.

Late in the spring when seniors have difficulty focusing on anything other than arrangements for the prom, I ask them to pull out these cumulative reading logs. The list includes no annotations, only the title, author, and date the book was completed. Inevitably, some students will have lost their lists (or never kept one in the first place). We take a few minutes to remind one another of the core works that most students read in ninth, tenth, and eleventh grade. I encourage everyone to add titles that they have read but never listed.

I then put the class into groups and offer them the following questions to stimulate their discussion. I remind them that I don't want answers to these questions but lively discussion. If they never get past talking about the first one, it probably means their book discussion has been a roaring success.

- Which of these books would you recommend to an incoming ninth grader as a "must read"?

- Which of these books do you think you might someday reread?

- Are there any books on this list that you still think about from time to time?

- If you had to choose one character from all of these books that you would most like to meet, who would it be?

When I see that their conversations are winding down, I ask students to take out their journals and write for ten minutes, describing how they think they have developed as readers since the ninth grade. Which books have been milestones for them? As readers, where do they plan to go from here?

Even students who have read very little seem to have something to say about this subject, particularly after their small-group discussions. Many students write about books that someone in their group just told them about and explain how they plan to read this next. Others lament that they know they haven't read as much as they should. Some blame teachers, but many more blame themselves. For most seniors the celebration of prom and graduation is tempered by the reality of what comes next: jobs, college, the armed services, babies. Students are responsive to this invitation to look backwards and then ahead to their future as readers.

Wayne Booth (1998) said, "When teachers are fully successful, they are successful beyond any of their conscious intentions about particular subjects: they make converts, they make souls that have been turned around to face a given way of being and moving in the world" (298). That's what I want to do. Make converts. I suppose the fourteen years I spent in Catholic schools may have something to do with this, but I see it as my mission in life to turn students into readers whose way of moving in the world is somehow shaped by classical literature. I want them to see their own lives as a hero's journey and to have learned from Odysseus and Bilbo Baggins that even when there seems to be no hope for survival, help will appear, though not always in the shape one might expect. I want them to have the courage to put themselves at risk—like Beowulf and Robin Hood—for the sake of others. I want their experience of reading *Crime and Punishment* to affect them so profoundly that they are never quite the same. My goal is to teach students how to read so well that their hearts beat with Raskolnikov's as he crouches inside the pawnbroker's apartment. I also want former students to feel vaguely sick when they go for too long without having read a good book.

I don't pretend to be fully successful in this endeavor. But the good sisters also taught me about optimism and perseverance. I know that seeds planted in ninth grade often do not bear fruit until much, much later.

The Power of Stories

Robert Scholes (1989) says, "Reading is not just a matter of standing safely outside texts, where their power cannot reach us. It is a matter of entering, of passing through the looking glass and seeing ourselves on the other side" (27). This is what reading does for me. It's what I also want for my students. Only a few weeks ago I experienced what Scholes describes while I was reading Virginia Woolf's *Mrs. Dalloway.* How I managed to earn a degree in English without ever having read this classic I will never know, but I came to the book these many years later through Michael Cunningham's Pulitzer Prize–winning novel *The Hours.* (If you have not yet read Cunningham's book, please put down this one right now and run to your local library or bookstore for a copy.)

One of the three intertwined stories in *The Hours* is a biographically accurate account of Virginia Woolf's life while she was writing

Mrs. Dalloway. As soon as I finished Cunningham's final page, I could not rest until I had read *Mrs. Dalloway.* I was indulging in one of my periodic reading binges, moving from book to book with an almost manic intensity.

Reading Mrs. Dalloway's musings, I passed through what Scholes describes as the looking glass of Woolf's text and found myself on the other side. For all the obvious differences of time, place, and dress, Clarissa and I have a lot in common. We are both creatures of enormous habit, making a virtue of these habits even when others view them as eccentricities. We both focus on details, even when this sometimes means missing the bigger picture. We both know how to throw a wonderful party.

Now I'm sure any Woolf scholar who happens to read what I've just written is likely to be saying, "What rubbish. Who cares about such personal drivel?" Well, readers care. In his book *Protocols of Reading*, Robert Scholes (1989) explains, "Reading is always, at once, the effort to comprehend and the effort to incorporate" (9). Readers are constantly engaged in both understanding the text and in connecting to it. One without the other is an incomplete reading.

Ten years from now this is the kind of reader I want my students to be. I want them to go on reading binges and know the feeling of needing a book as urgently as a thirsty man needs water. I want them to have the reading skills they need to negotiate any text, classic or contemporary. I want them to know what it feels like to step through the looking glass and see themselves in the characters they meet.

Inevitably, the day comes when the student must read or choose not to read without the lure of a grade or free pizza. My job as a literature teacher is to develop independence rather than dependence. I don't know a single teacher who makes house calls to former students struggling with a metaphor. They must learn to do for themselves.

CHAPTER FIVE

Of Excerpts and Allusions

The 1901 Ginn & Company sixth-grade literature textbook asserted in its introduction that

> Literature in its noblest form should do for the child what it does for the man — open the eyes to clearer vision, and nourish and inspire the soul. The reading book, therefore, has more direct influence upon the character of the pupil than any other text-book, and, with this in mind, it has been the fundamental purpose of this series to make its readers familiar with the best writers and their works. (Cyr 1901, 3)

Schools across the country spend billions of dollars on textbooks. Each year the anthologies seem to get bigger. Each year they are more expensive. Publishers offer a dazzling array of materials with flashy page design, gorgeous artwork, and lots of high-tech folderol. But before growing drunk on the package, the buyer should beware. Despite graphic advancements, the purposes of a literature text have not changed all that much since 1901.

The introduction to the Ginn & Company reader goes on to say

> We have been reading and becoming acquainted with the American poets; now we enter a new field of literature, and the great

prose writers, Hawthorne, Irving, Dickens, and Scott, with the English poet Tennyson, shed the influence of their characters and writings in the schoolroom. The pupil looks into their faces and visits their homes. Their early childhood, their battles with adversity, and the influences that determined the current of their lives become familiar. Then, with awakened interest and admiration, he reads the messages they have left behind them. (4)

One hundred years later I, too, want my students to have this experience.

When Instruction Lags Behind Development

It is interesting to note that the challenge of matching the student's reading ability and maturity with the text was no less a concern a hundred years ago than it is now: "Characteristic selections from these authors have been carefully chosen with reference to the capacity of the children" (4). Long before Lev Vygotsky (1962) formulated his zone of proximal development, educators were weighing the merits of literary texts against students' development as readers. Vygotsky believed that teachers should design instruction that challenges students to stretch. If lessons include only work that children can accomplish without the help of a teacher, students are being shortchanged. The thoughtful teacher aims instruction just beyond what students are able to perform independently.

> What the child can do in cooperation today he can do alone tomorrow. Therefore the only good kind of instruction is that which marches ahead of development and leads it; it must be aimed not so much at the ripe as at the ripening functions. (104)

Instruction is marching behind development in too many English classrooms. I believe we underestimate our students' capacity for comprehending complex literature. Persuaded by teenage complaints, we assign students an author's shorter novel regardless of its relative merit against a longer work: *Hard Times* instead of *Oliver Twist*; *Of Mice and Men* instead of *The Grapes of Wrath*, *The Old Man and the Sea* instead of *A Farewell to Arms*. Giving in to students' moans (which to my mind are developmentally appropriate and for that reason not to be heeded), we substitute serious literature with light, high-interest, easy-to-read books.

This is not to say that there isn't a place for light reading in everyone's life. I would be lost without my occasional fix from Patricia Cornwell or Elmore Leonard. But these are not the kind of texts that deserve the close scrutiny and probing discussions that a rigorous literature class is designed to promote. What I suggest as a solution to this dilemma of needing extended time to read within the school day as well as time for instruction and discussion is to have every student in middle and high school enrolled in two periods of English. One period would be reserved for silent, sustained reading and the other what we now consider their "English" class. Both would carry credit toward graduation. In the reading class students would be free to choose any book they like (this might be the text they have been assigned to read for homework in their English class or it might be a Stephen King novel) and to read for fifty uninterrupted minutes. Students would never have to write a book report or answer questions about what they read. Once a week, they might share with one another titles that they have enjoyed, but their reading would be otherwise undisturbed.

Twenty-five years at a comprehensive, public high school have taught me how difficult changes in the master schedule are to achieve. I have—and for the rest of my professional life at this school probably always will have—55 minutes a day with students. This works out to 275 instructional minutes a week. In every class apart from honors groups, I set aside 75 of these minutes weekly for reading. I don't carve out one day or the first 15 minutes of every day for this, but intersperse the reading time as needed within my instructional plan.

For example, when I think that students will find a chapter particularly difficult to get through, I ask them to read a page silently and then we talk about what we have read together. After a few minutes of discussion, we read another two pages. We talk some more. With each break, I extend the length of the passage to be read. This is far from a foolproof system because the very slowest readers have trouble keeping up whatever pace I set, but if I'm sensitive about not putting these individuals on the spot to respond to what they haven't yet read, students tell me that the exercise helps them keep going.

I wish I could simply assign thirty pages for homework reading and that every student would return the next day with the task completed. Without making excuses, many of my students' home lives preclude such a commitment to schoolwork. What I have found is that the more intentional I am about attaching the homework to class work, the more readily the work gets done. Sometimes this means reading during class and writing about what we read at home.

Shortchanged by Excerpts

Another way in which I believe that instruction is falling behind students' zone of proximal development is in its use of short excerpts to stand in for a writer's body of work. Not too long ago a colleague of mine had to leave school at the spur of the moment and asked me to baby-sit her American Literature class. I readily agreed and asked what they were reading. She hollered, "Thoreau" and dashed for the door.

"Wonderful," I thought. I love Thoreau and hadn't reread him for years. This afternoon was going to be fun. Well, it would have been fun if we had had before us anything that remotely resembled

Thoreau's writings. Instead of a coherent extended excerpt, the anthology that students were reading from offered snippets of Thoreau under headings like: "Solitude," "Nature," "Work." How could we discuss Thoreau's challenging ideas with only aphorisms to work from? I tried asking the discussion questions that followed each passage, but gave up when I couldn't figure out the answers either. There simply wasn't enough text to go on.

I told the students to close their books and allow me to read to them from a copy of *Civil Disobedience* that I had fortunately brought along. One student asked if all the things they were reading in their textbooks came from "real books like that." I wanted to cry. Thoreau Lite is worse than no Thoreau at all.

I recognize that for many schools and for many teachers literature anthologies make both economic and educational sense. New teachers should not be expected to construct a course in American literature from whole cloth; nor should teachers be spending precious preparation time at the Xerox machine. (Many of my colleagues and I will be spending several years in copyright purgatory. But at least we'll be together and can talk about books.) Literature anthologies also provide teachers with valuable background information on authors and offer good ideas for extended readings.

My complaint is with the selections themselves. I hate excerpts. One anthology that shall remain nameless actually published only the first third of a play. Huh? Why would anyone who cares about literature do such a thing? Did they anticipate that students would go out and buy a copy of the play to find out what happens to the characters next? I know I am ranting here, but it seems essential that works of literature should not be carved up, even given the limitations of a student's available reading time and the size of a publisher's page.

I don't just want my students to know who Thoreau is in order to be able to identify him correctly on a cultural literacy quiz; I want them to spend time at Walden Pond and get a bit drunk on

Thoreau's eloquent ways of thinking. The 1901 Ginn reader explains, "These selections have been somewhat abridged, but it has been thought wiser to have them a little longer than many text-books introduce, rather than to mar the symmetry and beauty of the author's work" (4). I completely agree.

Classical Literature in Contemporary Discourse

Speaking of cultural literacy, it is time to talk about the role classical literature plays in contemporary discourse. When students ask me why they need to read *The Odyssey* or *Julius Caesar,* I tell them facetiously that it is so they can understand *New Yorker* cartoons. Never having seen a copy of the magazine and unable to imagine why they ever would choose to, students look at me as though I have finally, truly lost my mind.

For years I have, with the help of students, collected cartoons with classical references. One of my favorites is the February 17, 1997 cover of *The New Yorker*, in which a love-struck monster stands by with flowers and valentine in hand as Victor Frankenstein prepares to throw the switch and bring to life an obviously female creature. I ask students to ponder how bereft they would be without the background information necessary to "read" this cover illustration. The clever ones remind me that Victor Frankenstein refused to create such a companion for the monster.

Throughout the school year I offer students extra credit (whatever that is since I never count points) for every classical reference they can find. One student brought in a Motorola pager ad with the message: "CAESAR—KEEP YOUR EYE ON BRUTUS—I'LL EXPLAIN LATER." We talked about whether Artemidorus might have used such a means to communicate with Caesar had pagers been available in ancient Rome.

During the Clinton impeachment proceedings, another student found a Paul Conrad political cartoon in which Kenneth Starr and

President Clinton are robed in Roman dress. A bloody body lies on the steps of the Capitol while a toga-clad elephant peeks from behind a column with a dripping dagger in its trunk. When George Stephanopoulos's exposé of the Clinton White House was published, a *Los Angeles Times* headline read, "Stephanopoulos Tells All; Critics Ask: Et Tu, George?"

My purpose in urging students to search for such classical references is to draw attention to their ubiquitous presence in contemporary discourse. I explain that writers and cartoonists use classical references as shorthand to comment on current conditions and characters. Editors count on the fact that their readers will have read certain well-known books and will have retained at least a vague memory of them.

A recent cover of *The New York Times Magazine* carried a picture of two babies, one a boy, the other a girl. "It's a . . . (your choice). A new sperm-splitting machine lets couples select a child's sex. All's well or Orwell?" The reference here is, of course, to George Orwell's *1984*. My students were quick to point out that a better choice would have been Aldous Huxley's *Brave New World*, where genetic engineering was the norm. Such examples of classical references demonstrate that it is not only bespectacled English teachers who know these books and characters, but most educated people. I posted several cartoons and advertisements with classical allusions on a bulletin board and then asked a group of tenth graders who had recently read *Julius Caesar* what they thought.

Spencer: I admit it's cute what that pager ad did, but isn't it really elitist? I mean, what if somebody never read *Julius Caesar* in school? Or what if they were absent that week?

Joe: Then they don't get the joke. I saw another one by that pager company that used the Wizard of Oz. Maybe the person looking at that version of the ad watches movies. Advertisers just want to grab your attention.

Me: That's a good point. Advertisers use references to connect their product to buyers. If one reference doesn't catch them, maybe another will. But why do you think the political cartoonist decided to cast Kenneth Starr and President Clinton as Antony and Caesar?

Joe: He's being really clever because he changes only one word of Antony's line but it makes all the difference.

Me: Antony opens his funeral oration with, "Friends, Romans, Countrymen. Lend me your ears. / I come to bury Caesar, not to praise him." Conrad has Starr saying, "I come to bury Clinton, not to censure him."

Nicole: I think Conrad wanted to make that same point Shakespeare made about Antony pretending to the people that he was only acting as a friend and not in fact trying to stir them up against the conspirators. Ken Starr pretends to be all official and without a personal axe to grind when really—

Joe: Exactly! Antony praises Caesar and Starr censures Clinton. Sorry, Nicole.

Nicole: What I was going to say was that Antony pretends to praise Brutus and Cassius by calling them "honorable men" but really he praises Caesar and makes Brutus and Cassius out to be murderers.

Spencer: But if you never read the play, the cartoon is pointless. I mean it makes us feel all smart because we see what the political cartoonist is doing, but what about everybody else?

Joe: Well, maybe they should read the play.

Spencer: You're a snob, Joe.

Me: No name-calling. What about Spencer's point? What do you think, Maryam?

Maryam: I think the cartoonist is trying to say something that is really complicated and that referring to *Julius Caesar* makes it easier for him to say what he wants to say. He thinks that the Republicans have stabbed Clinton in the back and that Starr really is out to bury the President. Can I show you this other cartoon I found?

Me: Of course. [The political cartoon, again by Paul Conrad, depicts a hand holding a skull with a bullet in it. The caption takes Hamlet's line, "Alas poor Yorick! I knew him, Horatio. . ." and substitutes Kosovo for Yorick.]

Maryam: I didn't understand it, but I was really upset about what was going on in Kosovo so I asked my older brother what it meant.

Me: Don't tell me, your brother was reading *Hamlet*.

Maryam: Yes. But I guess I want to support what Spencer was saying because that cartoon really made no sense at all to me and even after my brother explained about the gravedigger, I still didn't exactly understand. Maybe I will after I read the play.

To Open Their Eyes and Nourish Their Souls

Conversations like these help students begin to see that there is something enduring in the stories of Shelley and Shakespeare that writers and artists continue to draw from. I encourage students to argue about the potential elitism of literary references. I also want them to get the jokes. Over time I hope they will develop an awareness of the enduring things classics have to offer them as readers. For all our "progress" we find it hard to say it better than Shakespeare did.

Literature also allows journalists to frame their subject within a larger context and thereby lend greater significance to their message. In an essay critiquing the absence of African-American characters in the fall television lineup of programs, Howard Rosenberg (1999) makes reference to Ralph Ellison's *Invisible Man*.

"I am an invisible man," says the African-American narrator in one of this century's great novels, the one about a man whose black form fades into the darkness of the coal cellar where he lives. The hero of Ralph Ellison's *Invisible Man* goes on: "No. I am not a spook like those who haunted Edgar Allan Poe; nor am I one of your Hollywood-movie ectoplasms. I am a man of substance, of flesh and bone, fiber and liquids—and I might even be said to possess a mind. I am invisible, understand, simply because people refuse to see me."

Rosenberg goes on to describe the lineup of shows planned for the fall season and to point his finger at those responsible for deciding to omit African American characters from their casts. "Whether through sins of commission or omission, television has spent decades being pretty much an equal opportunity offender." Rosenberg concludes:

> All these years later too many minority members "of substance, of flesh and bone, fiber and liquids," still remain invisible on too much of TV, characters who, like Ralph Ellison's hero "might even be said to possess a mind." And based on these new fall shows, there's no cause for optimism.

Clearly it is possible to read Harold Rosenberg's essay without ever having read *Invisible Man*. But how much richer, how much more powerful his message becomes when coupled with the memory of Ellison's hero. It's the ability to tap that richness that I want my students to possess their whole lives long.

While I believe young adult fiction has a place in the recreational reading life of teenagers, I don't think these titles are the best choices when your goal is the study of literature. Few young adult books employ rich language or explore complex themes. The characters are often one-dimensional and almost always teenagers themselves. While students benefit enormously from small-group discussions about a YA book they have read in common, they don't need instructional guidance to get through the text. That's the beauty of young adult books! Instead of co-opting these titles for classroom use, let's keep putting them in students' hands for independent, pleasure reading.

I would like to make a final comparison between contemporary literature anthologies and the 1901 Ginn edition for twelve-year-olds. Could many middle school students today negotiate the work of Hawthorne, Dickens, Tennyson, Elliot, Browning, or Thackeray with any degree of success? Even Robert Louis Stevenson, long considered the staple of any boy's reading life, is heavy going for contemporary kids. While I am not recommending the return to an exclusive diet of nineteenth-century authors, and while celebrating the growing body of young adult literature available to teenage readers, I urge that the literature chosen for classroom study be of the finest quality. If the chosen texts are difficult for young readers, then we must address the problem of making students better readers, not fall back on simpler texts. Today, as in 1901, to "open their eyes to clearer vision and nourish and inspire their souls" is an enormous task. I need the work of giants in hand to help me.

CHAPTER SIX

Learning from the Inside Out How Stories Work

Walking in a writer's shoes can be a powerful way for students to learn about classical literature from the inside out. Some students are adept at counting beats and marking accents, but others find imitation a more powerful way to understand meter. If students are unsure how Iambic pentameter works, ask them to imitate a line of Shakespeare's, inserting words of their own in place of the bard's, following his rhythmic pattern. For example, students can take "The quality of mercy is not strain'd; / It droppeth as the gentle rain from heaven / Upon the place beneath" (*Merchant of Venice*, act 4, scene 1) and then use these lines to describe the quality of another virtue or vice. They might produce "The quality of ardor is not cold; / It burneth as the coals of hell / Inside a lover's heart" or "The quality of hatred is not black; / It shineth as the brightest light from one / Who loathes to another."

Imitation or modeling also works for other aspects of form and style. I struggled for years trying to teach students about epic similes, extended comparisons that intensify the heroic stature of characters and events. Then I stumbled upon the idea of having students choose one of Homer's epic similes and adapt it to describe how they perform an ordinary act. I suggested they consider:

- How they practice an instrument
- How they struggle on a test
- How they sit in front of TV
- How they eat a banana
- How they work out for a sport

Of course, students come up with better ideas than mine, but they often need examples to get started. On occasion I have in my file a simile written by the older brother or sister of someone in my current class. Reading these papers never fails to make kids smile.

Tenth grader Brian Ziff wrote, "As a hundred-year-old man stabs with withered fingers that bear the fork for a remaining pea on his plate, so did heavy-eyed, soccer-sore Brian pick at his godly Corn Flakes." His classmate Manisha Parekh crafted, "As a mouse scurries back to its hole, chased by a cat, and fearful for its life, so did Manisha scramble about her messy room, gathering her papers for school." Modeling their own lines after Homer's, these students had internalized both the structure and the point of epic similes. They could see how a poet draws from subjects the listener or reader is familiar with—such as a man eating peas or a mouse scurrying away from a cat—to describe what is unfamiliar: how tired Brian felt, how quickly Manisha had to move. Students now knew not only how Homer did what he did but why.

Modeled After the Masters

Students are wonderful imitators. Once I saw how easily the epic similes were flowing, I asked them to use Homer's invocation to the muse as a model for the opening of an epic poem they might write someday about their odyssey through high school. For the moment we would be writing only the first page. I intended for this to be more than a creative writing exercise. I wanted them to play with language, but I also knew that many were struggling to make sense of this epic poem. I thought that appropriating Homer's lines for their own use would help students negotiate his language with greater ease. Joe Green, a tenth grader on the school's water polo team, penned the following adaptation from Albert Cook's 1967 translation.

> Tell me, Muse about the too-much-to-do Joe
> who for many night was sleepless with all work and no play
> In the pool he suffered many cramps in his legs,
> Striving for a life and his companions' return.
> But he could not find his companions,
> for they were all out bowling.

Along with having a bit of fun, these students were experimenting with seeing their own lives in a heroic context. They were also learning how to parody. Isn't this one of the reasons we teach these classic stories? As Matthew Arnold so eloquently describes in "*Buried Life*":

> But often, in the world's most crowded streets,
> But often, in the din of strife,
> There rises an unspeakable desire
> After the knowledge of our buried life;
> A thirst to spend our fire and restless force
> In tracking out our true, original course;
> A longing to inquire
> Into the mystery of this heart which beats
> So wild, so deep in us—to know
> Whence our lives come and where they go.

Teenagers, despite being caught up in the superficial concerns of appearance and who likes whom, worry deeply about their lives and where their lives will go. When I offer students this invitation to describe something they experience every day in elevated language, they begin to see how they, like Odysseus, have embarked on a journey of self-discovery. Dalia Yerushalmi, a talented violinist in the school orchestra, offered this invocation:

> Tell me, Muse, about the girl of many notes,
> Who many hours practiced when she joined
> Mr. Schwabe's Symphony Orchestra.
> She saw many staff, and knew their notes;
> With her violin she suffered many pains within her heart,
> Striving for the day when she would be in tune.

I particularly liked the way students instinctively chose to write about an area of their lives in which they were struggling. The mock-serious tone they adopted seemed to allow the writers both to gripe about their problems and to see these problems as archetypal obstacles that clutter every hero's path to glory.

The Hero with a Thousand Faces

In *The Hero with a Thousand Faces,* Joseph Campbell (1973) explains how the mythological hero ventures forth from the ordinary world into unexplored territory. There the hero meets unimagined obstacles, monsters with unthinkable powers, ogres who—on a bad day—may look much like the water polo coach or orchestra director. But the hero overcomes these obstacles, garnering a scar or two along the way, and ultimately triumphs, returning to the ordinary world with newfound knowledge.

Of course, few teenagers identify themselves as "heroes" or make the connection between their own messy lives and a hero's journey without some prompting. I show them Peter Stillman's (1985) definition of a hero:

To honor an individual with the exalted title of hero, we must be satisfied (although not always consciously so) that he has performed certain ritualized tasks and feats. Furthermore, his character must be essentially noble, although not unflawed. A hero must leave behind him, or overcome, the weaknesses and temptations we give in to, or his quest is doomed to failure. He must suffer privations, dangers and agonies beyond those we believe we're able to endure—even if he suffers them in connection with an apparently meaningless quest. Furthermore, he must act out his role alone. Although a hero figure may be surrounded by others, his is a spiritual solitude; as he moves deeper into the unknown, his solitude deepens too. (31–32)

We talk about heroes they have met in fairy tales, in literature, and in the movies who seem to meet Stillman's guidelines. It is often important at this point to make the distinction between "real life" heroes who run into burning buildings to save babies and archetypal heroes. I want students to think about how archetypal heroes point the way for the rest of us.

Kjerstin Barrett's imitation of the beginning of Book II of *The Odyssey* situates her within this heroic context. Drawing from her experiences in marching band, Kjerstin demonstrates how she has suffered privations and agonies and ultimately triumphs.

And when the early-born, rosy-fingered dawn appeared,
The dear daughter of Chester jumped from her bed
Drew around her many layers of clothing for warmth,
Slung the heavy tuba over her shoulder and
The much-encrusted marching shoes beneath her aching feet,
And went out onto the field, like a zombie to look at.
At once Mr. Sakow ordered the drum majors with their piercing voices
To summon the musically-challenged band members to rehearse.

> The drum majors made summons, but the weary students moved
> slowly.
> Kjerstin set the brass tuba on her sloping shoulder.
> Not alone, but the lazy-footed marchers went along with her.
> If only Athene would have shed a divine grace about her now.
> Mr. Sakow, a man bent from many marching seasons,
> Raised his baton, and then music was all we were.

I was so impressed with what students had done that I created a display in the main office titled "Recently Discovered Fragments of Epic Poetry." It made a great hit at Open House. Parents loved seeing their children imitating Homer rather than an MTV announcer.

Learning in a State of Flow

Ashlee Henderson struggled whenever she had to tackle an essay assignment. So it came as a surprise to both of us when we discovered that she found epic poetry easier to generate than analytical prose. Reading her imitation of Homer, I saw how much I had underestimated Ashlee's insight into what she read. Judging from the way she developed an argument, I assumed her understanding of the literature we had been reading was very limited. However, looking at what she wrote here I could see how deeply Ashlee had internalized Homer's poetry. Comparing herself with Odysseus's struggling son Telemachos, Ashlee reveals how clearly she sees the obstacles this young hero faced as well as those she herself faces daily:

> And when the early-born, rosy-fingered dawn appeared,
> The body of Ashlee rose without her soul,
> Took a quick shower, ate breakfast,
> And went out of her room like a harpy to look at.

At once she ordered her parents to summon
The light-haired siblings to breakfast.
The parents made summons, and they quickly gathered together.
And when they were gathered she went to the table
Holding her hairbrush in her fist,
not alone but the sturdy barrettes came, too.
Morever Mrs. Jago had shed a divine grace around her.
The family marveled as she sat down in her father's seat
And the light-haired siblings gave way.
Then the designated carpool mom arrived
A woman bent with age who knew numberless things
She too had dear daughters who went with bright-eyed Ashlee
In the hollow minivan to Santa Monica High, abounding in
    teenagers.
Jennifer had been killed by the savage principal in the hallowed
    halls
And another daughter Kacey fell in with the drug crowd.
Two daughters stayed always in their father's mansion
But still she remembered the lost ones in grief and sorrow.
For them she wept and then addressed the family:
"Listen to me now, family, in what I say.
We have not once met for much too long
And now who has called us together? And to which of the young
    women
Or of those who are older, has there come so great a need?"

When I talked with Ashlee about what she had written, she said that this piece just seemed to "come to her," that the words just "kinda flowed." I thought of Mihaly Csikszentmihalyi's (1990) theory of flow and began to see a possible explanation for Ashlee's newly found source of power. Csikszentmihalyi posits that a person can become so involved in work or in an activity that nothing else seems to matter. He calls this the theory of optimal experience. When caught up in a state of "flow," a person finds the work itself so enjoyable that distractions and even time disappear. Intensely involved, the person will often continue the work even at great cost, simply for the sheer pleasure of doing it. Csikszentmihalyi explains:

> Contrary to what we usually believe, the best moments in our lives are not the passive, receptive, relaxing times—although such experiences can also be enjoyable, if we have worked hard to attain them. The best moments usually occur when a person's body or mind is stretched to its limits in a voluntary effort to accomplish something difficult and worthwhile. (3)

Imagine if we could transform schoolwork into a series of flow-producing activities. Imagine moving students from a position of resistance to reading difficult and worthwhile books to Csikszentmihalyi's state of optimal experience. Homer's stories have the potential to illuminate lives. Reading *The Odyssey* may not be what most kids think of when urging one another to "go with the flow," but they might be surprised to discover how pleasurable time spent with this master storyteller can be.

Ashlee continued to produce her best work when assignments invited her to make connections between her own life and her schoolwork. For a project in which students were asked to create a metaphor for education using a small, empty box, Ashlee made a ceramic brain and mounted it atop the box. She called her piece "Thinking Outside the Box." Ashlee's analytical writing began to reflect an integration of her creative and intellectual sides toward the very end of the year, following the sobering experience of being suspended from school. Looking back at the Homeric imitation that she had written in October, I thought about how Ashlee seemed to have had an intimation of what an odyssey her tenth-grade year was going to be.

Stimulating Your Many-Minded Students

Another feature of epic poetry that students often find odd—and, as a result, creates a stumbling block to their reading—is Homer's use of epithets. Epithets are short, stock words or phrases that are attached to most names and places. The purpose of epithets is two-fold. They provide a quick thumbnail sketch of a character or setting for readers as well as allowing singers to take a short mental break while recalling what comes next in the story.

For homework during our first few days reading *The Odyssey*, I asked students to make a list of all the epithets they could find in the text. When they returned to class, students shared from their lists. In Book III they found: bronze-covered heaven; grain-giving earth; bright-eyed goddess Athene; aegis-bearing Zeus; two-handled cup; wine-faced sea. I realized that they didn't recognize epithets that take the form of an appositive, as in "Nestor, breaker of horses" or "Nestor, the Gerenian horseman."

Once students had the sound of an epithet in their heads, I invited them to create a few of their own. I asked the class—assuring them and making them pledge to one another that everything they wrote would stay within these four walls—to write an epithet for their least favorite teacher, their mother or father, their best friend, their pet, a movie star, a figure in the news, the President, and our principal. Students enjoy the exercise so much that they almost forget they are studying poetry. While they are in this state of "flow," we return to the text.

Along with teaching students about epithets from the inside out, I was also sending students the message that Homer didn't compose as he did simply to make life more difficult for tenth graders. Sometimes it seems that students believe classical authors purposely create obstacles for readers. While this is an unexamined belief in most teenagers' minds, it is nonetheless a powerful one. I want students to see how Homer played with language for the sheer pleasure he took in words. He was probably in what Mihaly Csikszentmihalyi would call a state of flow.

Freedom to Teach, Freedom to Read

Studying stories from the inside out can also be a way for teachers and students to think their way through censorship challenges. Often when individuals object to books like *Catcher in the Rye* or *The Color Purple*, it is on the basis of particular lines or expressions that some find offensive. The more our students understand character motivation, historical context, and diction at the service of tone, the better they will be able to articulate to anyone intent upon protecting them from such books why the author chose to employ this language. I believe that strong, thoughtful students are one of the best defenses against censorship.

Rather than avoiding particular books to stave off the headache and heartache of a challenge, teachers should develop clear rationales for the literature they teach. Fortunately much of the work has been done for us. The National Council of Teachers of English in partnership with the International Reading Association has created a compact disc called *Rationales for Challenged Books*. The CD-ROM was written primarily for middle and high school teachers and includes more than two hundred rationales. Of the books listed in Chapter 1, fifteen can be found on this disk, along with references to reviews, plot summaries, redeeming qualities, teaching objectives, and model assignments.

I always encourage new teachers in the English department to read through the NCTE/IRA rationales before they begin teaching *Black Boy, The Adventures of Huckleberry Finn, Catcher in the Rye, Their Eyes Were Watching God,* or *I Know Why the Caged Bird Sings.* Often understanding why someone might object to a piece of literature helps a teacher construct her own personal rationale for teaching a particular book. Most challenges begin with a phone call from a parent. If the teacher who responds to that call can articulate a thoughtful explanation of why the book is being studied and then offer the student alternate selections, the problem is often diffused.

Another excellent resource for teachers is the summer 1997 issue of the journal of the Colorado Language Arts Society (CLAS), *Statement,* which focuses on rationales for challenged materials. Copies are available from NCTE. In her introduction, editor Louann Reid (1997) explains that:

> Paradoxically, it may take a village to raise a child, but it seems to take only one complaint to raze a curriculum. Reports from organizations such as People for the American Way and the American Library Association demonstrate that challenges to teaching materials and methods are increasing—and are increasingly successful. Members of the Executive Committee of the Colorado Language Arts Society join thousands of others who are concerned about encroachments on the freedom of expression, the students' right to read, and intellectual freedom. (2)

The CLAS Executive Committee formulated a position statement regarding academic freedom that I believe can serve as a model for any school district in this country. For that reason, I have included it here in its entirety.

On Academic Freedom and Professional Responsibility

The Colorado Language Arts Society declares that society is best served by an education system that promotes the robust exchange of ideas. The freedom to study, to inquire, and to explore new ideas is fundamental to a healthy education.

Experience has shown that there are a number of things that educators can do to create the best educational experiences for their students, to maintain a healthy relationship with the school community, and to minimize the extent of any controversies over materials used for instruction.

The Colorado Language Arts Society affirms that professional educators should use their expertise to select instructional materials and experiences that they believe will advance the education goals they have identified for their students. CLAS also affirms the joint statement of NCTE and IRA that states, "All students in public school classrooms have the right to materials and educational experiences that promote open inquiry, critical thinking, diversity in thought and expression, and respect for others. Denial or restriction of this right is an infringement of intellectual freedom."

Educators have a unique influence on their students. Thus, CLAS also affirms that with academic freedom come the following responsibilities:

1. Educators have a responsibility to take into account the age, maturity, and readiness of their students as they select instructional materials.

2. Educators have a responsibility to learn about and follow their districts' policies and procedures in selecting and using educational materials.

3. Educators have a responsibility to become aware of and understand the diverse standards and values of their communities.

4. Educators have a responsibility to develop education plans and rationales for the use of specific classroom materials, including nonprint, print, and multi-media materials, exercises, and assignments. (1996)

Louann Reid with Jamie Hayes Neufeld has also edited a book called *Rationales for Teaching Young Adult Literature* that addresses important concerns of anyone who puts books in students' hands. It is an invaluable resource for appropriate titles as well as for advice about defending these titles against challenges.

Every teacher should expect, at some time in his or her career, to face a textbook challenge. While the circumstances of the challenge and the nature of the objections may be outside a teacher's control, there is much we can do to defend our students' right to read and our own right to teach. My best advice is not to go it alone. Help is always available from the National Council of Teachers of English, the International Reading Association, and the American Library Association.

CHAPTER SEVEN

Testing That Teaches

As I have indicated previously, every time teachers of literature give an objective test , they undermine their students' confidence in themselves as readers. The very act of posing questions whose answers will be judged as correct or incorrect sends wrong messages to students: that there is only one right answer, that their teacher is the source of all correct information in a classroom, and that the purpose of reading is to answer questions. Unless this set of beliefs is what we want to encourage, we must abandon all tests forever.

Objective Tests Only Tell Us What We Already Know

If my goal is to create a community of readers and writers, peopled with students who can and do read and write, it does not make sense for me to ask my students to match "Penelope" with the description "Odysseus's long-suffering and faithful wife." If any of my students do not know this matching fact after the class has spent three to four weeks reading the epic, I would hope that I already know this from my ongoing assessment of the students' class participation (or lack thereof). Why punish those students by putting them through the ordeal of an objective test—and possibly unintentionally encouraging them to cheat—when I should already have more than enough information to assign a grade? Why waste valuable class time this way? If you doubt that this is true, the next time you give an objective test, jot down how you think each student will do before you correct the tests. I'll wager there will be few surprises.

Objective Tests Encourage Competition Instead of Collaboration

Objective tests also foster a competitive spirit in the classroom. Test scores encourage students to label one another as "smarter-than-me" or "dumber-than-me," an attitude that results in severely circumscribed classroom discussion. Consider this categorization from a student's point of view: it's hard to feel good about contributing to a discussion on Monday when you have just been handed a flaming red D from Friday's quiz.

Teachers contradict themselves when, in one breath, they tell students to say what they think about a piece of literature, and in the next, ask them to fill in the name of Victor Frankenstein's father on an objective test. Often even the most astute readers will find they can't remember this level of detail off the top of their heads. Does making grade percentage distinctions between readers who can recall plot details encourage students to read more thoughtfully? I think not. Students feel no ownership of information presented on a multiple-choice test. Even when they are asked to construct questions and submit them as items for an exam, students tend to imitate the superficial questions they have seen so many times before.

Just as when students write they need to feel confident enough to use their own ideas in their essays, when students read, they need to have the confidence to share their interpretations with others. Ideally, every voice will have weight and substance and will add to the group's collective understanding of the text. For this to happen, however, students must respect one another's varied interpretations and regard one another as thinkers. There can be no "dummies" in this type of classroom. The pecking order among teenagers is a horrible thing to witness. It causes students both to silence themselves and to close their ears to anyone who looks or thinks differently from them. Teachers are relatively powerless to influence this behavior outside the classroom. Inside the classroom, however, we have the power either to reinforce the status quo or to establish a different kind of order, one where powerful ideas rule.

I had a terrible situation in a class last year. One student could not open his mouth without at least four other boys jeering. Matt, a very bright and thoughtful tenth grader, did have difficulty expressing himself and tended to circle around his point for several minutes before stating it, but he also often saw what everyone else was missing. I came down hard on the boys for their rudeness but was not satisfied that even when they stopped they were doing anything more than obeying me. What I wanted was for them to see how much they needed Matt's thinking as a complement to their own. Then I came up with the idea to put these five young men in a group with a difficult literary problem to solve. They were to explain to the class how Paul in Erich Maria Remarque's *All Quiet on the Western Front* was metaphorically torn in two. Without Matt, these boys were in danger of looking like fools. Suddenly they hung on his every word, asking him questions, listening to and copying out his sometimes tedious answers. Their presentation (with someone other than Matt as spokesperson) was excellent.

Objective Tests Are Not College Prep

Some argue that objective testing prepares students for college, yet the students who go on to do well at the university level are those who read widely with understanding, who speak articulately about what they have read, and who write with confidence. Objective tests don't develop any of these qualities in learners.

Questions are the key to understanding literature. Student must have space to ask real questions, ones they genuinely want answers to. Demanding their quick response to objective test questions discourages such thinking about literature. Besides, the issues we choose to emphasize—for example, the differences between Brutus's and Cassius's rhetorical styles—may not be what fascinated a student when reading *Julius Caesar*. That particular reader may have been more interested in the political power struggle between Antony and Octavius; therefore, this is what that reader remembered. A teacher constructing an objective test would be, in effect, punishing the Antony/Octavius reading while rewarding those who matched the teacher's Brutus/Cassius reading. It is obvious how unfair this approach is, regardless of whether you can justify it by saying, "But we talked about the funeral orations in class." Our job as literature teachers should be to model reading and thinking about a text, not to dictate meaning. Because objective tests deny students their right to a defensible interpretation, they actually discourage both reading and thinking.

Objective tests do a tremendous disservice to anyone who is trying to bring the real world of reading and writing into the classroom. Take a moment to think about the last book you read. What stayed with you? It is probably neither the characters' names nor a short identification tag about them. What stayed with you is probably a feeling for the book, a message the author conveyed especially to you, a world you walked in for the period of time you read. How would you feel about taking a test on this story and answering true-or-false questions about what happened or what the book meant?

I know such a test would severely undermine the pleasure I took from the last book I read, José Saramago's *Blindness*. Although I finished the novel only yesterday, I could not with certainty tell you the main characters' names. Does this make me a poor reader? Should I be punished for remembering the haunting narrative voice rather than the name of the city where the story took place? Though I am itching to talk with someone about the book, I do not want to have to match my reading of it with anyone else's. For someone—anyone, even the author—to be set up as the arbiter of what a book says to a reader contradicts everything we know about reading. Why would I practice in my classroom that which I do not believe is true in the "real" world?

An Alternative to Objective Tests

The challenge to those who object to such tests is to devise ways of assessing students' reading that actually teach them more about what they have read. I want to stretch their understanding. To assess a class of tenth graders on their reading of *The Odyssey*, I asked them to write about a major character in the epic who was most like them and to explain the similarity using examples from their own and the character's lives. Here is Karen Montoya's response.

> Zeus-born, son of Laertes, Odysseus of many devices resembles me the most out of all the characters in *The Odyssey*. I can relate to him because in the whole epic his purpose is to see his family and someday reach sunny Ithaca. Like Odysseus, I am often sad because I know what it is like for one's family to be so far away, mine being in Mexico. I don't have to go through the dangerous adventures Odysseus experiences, but I do have to wait a long time before seeing them again.
>
> When in the land of Phaecians, a singer comes to town and relates the story of the battle at Troy, Odysseus' own story. Odysseus shed a tear, trying to hide it from the hospitable Phaecians. A couple of weeks ago I saw a television show about Puebla, Mexico, what I call my land. It showed the town's churches and schools and the town square. These things are part of my story and my life. It made me sad to be so far away, and I cried. Odysseus and I grieve when each hears his own story.

Reading this essay left no doubt in my mind that Karen had (1) read the book and (2) understood what she read. As well as achieving these primary assessment goals, the prompt gave her an opportunity for further learning by inviting her to see the heroic dimension of her own life. This does not happen when students match names with quotes or identify true-or-false statements.

Class results on this "test" did not fall in a bell-shaped curve because many more students were successful than a grade distribution chart would predict. Does this mean I abandoned rigor in my teaching? Not to me it doesn't. Karen's analysis of Odysseus demonstrates recall of details, reading comprehension, and insight into character motivation. The fact that such achievement was possible for most of the class should be cause for celebration. Student success should be our goal, not a cause for worry about grade inflation.

In one unsuccessful paper, a boy compared himself with Achilles solely on the basis of their shared strength and bravery. While applauding his strong self-image, I was critical of the absence of supporting evidence from the Trojan War or from Achilles' visit with Odysseus in the underworld. Such a prompt does separate those who have read a text with care from those who have not.

What I discovered as I read these essays was the relationship students had developed with the text—for some a passing acquaintance, for others a bond. This is the information I need to assess the appropriateness of a particular book as well as the quality of my instruction. I was also able to measure the commitment of students as readers and writers. What more could I ask of an evaluation instrument?

Unconventional Assessment

Last spring when my seniors had finished reading *Crime and Punishment,* I was at a bit of a loss for how to assess their reading. We had had such powerful discussions about the book that I didn't need to check for understanding. They already had a paper due Friday concerning their outside reading, so I was reluctant to assign another essay. I fumbled around for a while, and then had one of my best ideas in years. Since it would require introducing a seemingly unrelated piece of literature, I begged my students to indulge me. I promised it would all make sense in the end.

What we did was turn to Wallace Stevens' poem "Thirteen Ways of Looking at a Blackbird." As always, students were puzzled but enchanted by Stevens' language. For homework I asked them to write a poem, modeled after Stevens', titled "Thirteen Ways of Looking at Raskolnikov."

The next day I asked if anyone would like to read what he or she had written, hoping a brave few would volunteer. Almost every hand went up. What followed was an extraordinary display of these students' personal and private interpretations of Dostoevsky's novel. I wish I could include every one of them here. If you haven't read Wallace Stevens' poem in a long time, treat yourself to a rereading before you peruse these students' poems.

Cynthia Luo is the youngest of three sisters. The first two were both valedictorians at Santa Monica High School. When she wrote this poem, Cynthia was going through a very difficult time working through the fact that a B in Calculus was going to mean she could not follow in her sisters' footsteps. Cynthia's home language is Chinese.

Thirteen Ways of Looking at Raskolnikov

1
Among twenty snowy mountains
The only moving things
Were the eyes of Raskolnikov

2

He was of three minds
Like an axe
On which there was
The smear of three people's blood.

3

The guilt is nothing
The suffering is everything

4

A man and two women
Are three.
A man and two women and an axe
Are one.

5

He does not know which is more revolting
The repugnance of the blood
And gore spilt by his hands
Or the memory of them

6

A red shadow on the floor
Has an undecipherable cause

7

O thin men of Petersburg
Why do you imagine murderous painters?
Do you not see how Raskolnikov
Walks among you?

8

He knows noble accents
And lucid, inescapable rhythms;
But he knows, too,
That the painter is not involved
In what he knows.

9

When Raskolnikov fled the scene,
It marked the beginning
Of the suffering he would endure

10

At the sound of Raskolnikov's sighs
Even the pawnbroker's customers
Would cry out sharply

11

He rode over Connecticut
In a glass coach.
Once, a fear pierced him,
In that he thought
What on earth was he doing
In Connecticut, so far away from Russia

12

Sonia is crying
Raskolnikov must be lying

13

It was evening all afternoon
It was sunny

And it was about to be sunny
Raskolnikov sat
In the cedar-limbs of Pofiry's chair

Though Anna Altshuler lived in Russia until she was nine and continues to speak Russian at home, her access to Dostoevsky was through English. Needless to say, her parents were very pleased that we read this novel that had been so much a part of their education.

Thirteen Ways of Looking at Raskolnikov

1
Among twenty bustling taverns
The only moving thing
Was the mind of Raskolnikov.

2
I was of three minds
Like one in delirium
Like Raskolnikov.

3
Raskolnikov in the summer heat
Is only a small part of God's work

4
Crime and punishment
Are one.
Crime and punishment and redemption
Are one.

5
I do not know which to prefer

———

Being extraordinary
Or being ordinary
The ability to kill
Or the ability to love

6

He swung the axe.
The blood gushed
As from an overturned glass.
The mood traced in the shadow
An indecipherable cause.

7

O thin men of St. Petersburg
Why do you dream about Lazarus?
Why do you not see how hopelessness
Entangles the feet
Of the children about you?

8

I know noble accents
And lucid, inescapable rhythms;
And I know, too,
That I am capable
Of experiencing Raskolnikov's fate.

9

When Raskolnikov left society
He could feel free in prison.

10

At the sight of Raskolnikov
Roaming in the darkness

Even strangers cry out
"Murderer! Murderer!"

11

He rode over to Siberia
With an unquiet mind.
Once, a fear pierced him
In that he mistook
His own shadow
For Napoleon.

12

Life continues.
Raskolnikov must find redemption.

13

It was night all nine years
It was dark
And it was going to be dark
Until it was allowed
For there to be light.

Nura Sadeghpour is an intense student. She said little during our class discussion of *Crime and Punishment* (with thirty-eight students in the class, it may have been difficult to get a word in), but her body language made me feel that she was thoroughly engaged in our work with the novel. When she read this poem, I knew for sure.

Thirteen Ways of Looking at Raskolnikov

1

On the dark, sinister staircase
The only moving things
Were the legs of Napoleon.

2

He was of three minds
Literally.

3

The door rattled in the silence
It was a small part of the punishment.

4

A man and two women
Are one.
A murderer and a prostitute
And an axe and a Bible
Are one.

5

I do not know which to detest more,
A drunken axe-murderer
Or a drunken scholar.

6

There is no window
And if there were there would be no glass.
The shadow of a man
Crosses in and out, to and fro
The couch
Traces the outline of his body
Where he spends half his day.

7

Oh extraordinary Russian mouse
Do you not see how the cat
Purrs with pouncing games on his mind?

———

8

I know noble accents
And lucid, inescapable rhythms;
But I know, too,
that one's lips taste like dirt
After kissing the ground.

9

When blood is shed
It leaves its mark
On a pair of dirty socks

10

At the moment
When dark flied to light
The truth will astound,
And confuse.

11

He sent himself to Siberia
On a half-dying mule.
Once, a fear nagged him
And he mistook
The shadow of his equipage
For a beautiful stallion.

12

The women are dead.
Someone must have killed them.

13

It was evening all the way through.
It was snowing

There was no snow on the ground.
The convict sat in his cell.
Free.

While Cynthia, Anna, and Nura's poems are extraordinary examples of student work that demonstrate their own gifts for language, every student in the class generated a thoughtful poem. Some borrowed heavily from Stevens' lines. Others were technically inept. But whatever their merit as poems, these responses demonstrated a deep and abiding response to *Crime and Punishment*. All I could do was scribble in my grade book: "Among thirty-eight senior students / The only thing not moving / Was their awestruck, lucky teacher."

The Essay as Experiment

The most common way that I assess student learning is through essays. I believe student essayists should work in the style of Michel de Montaigne. Fed up with sixteenth-century discourse, Montaigne experimented with a new form of personal writing. He knew that what he was creating fit no traditional category so he simply called what he produced *essais*, meaning attempts, or trials, or experiments. I want my students' essays to be experiments in thinking.

In his introduction to *The Norton Book of Personal Essays*, Joseph Epstein (1997) describes the essay as a form of discovery:

> I sometimes make notes recalling anecdotes, facts, oddities of one kind or another that I wish to include in an essay, but where precisely in the essay they will be used I cannot say in advance. As for a previous design or ultimate goal for my essays, before I write them I have neither. The personal essay is, in my experience, a form of discovery. What one discovers in writing such essays is where one stands on complex issues, problems,

questions, subjects. In writing the essay, one tests one's feelings, instincts, thoughts in the crucible of composition. (15)

I love that phrase, "the crucible of composition." Clearly student writers need more guidance and structure than an accomplished essayist like Epstein, but I fear that if we nail students to an artificial structure like the five-paragraph essay, they will never know the intellectual joy of discovering what they think as they write. I am not suggesting that we allow students to turn in whatever random thoughts appear as they compose at their computer screen. Good writing must be carefully crafted and responded to. But the best writing is always inspired.

Often I have students construct their own focus questions. Other times I write prompts. Always I give them choices. The following essay prompts have resulted in interesting student essays:

An Essay on an Epic

Please write an essay in response to one of these questions. Use your books and your notes, but most of all your brains.

1. Epics focus on the heroism of one person who exists as a symbol of strength, virtue, and courage in the face of conflict. Discuss.

2. The epic poem is meant to enhance the reader's sense of good and evil. Discuss.

3. Epics enable their audiences to understand the past and to control their own destiny through the inspiration of the poem's noble ideas. Discuss.

Inevitably a student or two will approach me with a different idea for how they would like to write about the epic they have read. I press the student to explain to me why theirs is a compelling idea, but I never say no. My prompts are only offered as possible ways to approach their essay, jumping-off places for their own thinking.

Unfortunately, some teachers cling to more rigid forms of the essay and to objective tests for the power they allow teachers to wield over students. But this is not a real power, and students know it. Real power resides in the literature—the power to move us and make us more than what we have been. It is to this end that I teach, to show students the joy of being so moved. In my class, we do not have time for five-paragraph essays and multiple-choice tests; we have too much real reading and writing and talking to do.

CHAPTER EIGHT

Film Versions of the Classics: To View or Not to View?

What I am going to say is likely to upset some readers. To assist those who may want to skip this chapter, I will declare my position immediately: Despite the plethora of extraordinary versions of classics available on video, I think English teachers should be very careful about using class time to show films.

Language Arts Standards on Viewing

Most of the forty-nine states that have adopted language arts standards (only Iowa has chosen not to) have included references to viewing in their list of standards. Along with the familiar language arts of reading, writing, listening, and speaking, viewing and visual representation have been added as essential language arts skills. Just as the *Standards for the English Language Arts* written by the National Council of Teachers of English and the International Reading Association do, state documents recommend that students go beyond seeing film versions of the texts they read and that they study visual texts in their own right.

I applaud this expansion of the language arts, particularly in an age when children are bombarded daily with seductive visual images. Every time they gaze at television, computer, or movie screens, children must exercise judgement. Teaching them about the ploys of advertising and the power of a visual image to affect viewers is essential. I also believe that the study of film as genre is an important and lasting aspect of a liberal arts education. *But instruction in viewing and film should not occur in an English class.*

Making the Most of Precious Class Time

Every moment in an English class is precious. In earlier chapters I criticized reading aloud to students as a waste of classroom minutes that should instead be spent talking about what students have read at home. I feel the same way about showing movies. By the time a teacher has taken attendance, made a few announcements, and tuned in the VCR, only about forty minutes of a typical class period are left for the movie. This means that the average feature film will take three class periods to show. If a teacher shows five movies in a school year (which, given the number of excellent film adaptations now available doesn't seem unreasonable), students will have lost fifteen days or three weeks of class time to "viewing." In a typical school year of 180 days, these students will have spent 8 percent of their class time in front of the TV passively viewing. I do not believe this is a wise use of their time. Too often when the lights go down and the monitor lights up, teenagers hit their internal relax button and shut down all critical faculties. Some pull out their calculators and start their math homework. A few put their heads down for a snooze. However the lesson has been framed, most students consider a period watching a movie as a period off.

Teachers unintentionally foster this attitude by scheduling films for days when they must be out of class. The number of lesson plans that read "Show film" is legion. Substitute teachers don't mind because it doesn't take much effort to press the PLAY button. Kids don't mind because they aren't being asked to do any work. And the day's lesson plan was easy to write. What can never be recovered is one hour in the education of a child.

A better use of student time when the teacher is absent is to have the substitute divide the class into small groups and hand out selected passages from the previous night's reading for the group to teach to their classmates. When I know that I am going to be out of my classroom, I micromanage this activity, assigning particular students to particular groups to help the substitute teacher maintain order. I make copies of the passages I want groups to become experts on so that they can annotate the excerpt as they reread. I also suggest the following strict time line for the substitute to follow:

- Give students five minutes to reread and annotate their passage. This should be a silent activity.

- Give students ten minutes to discuss what they think are the important ideas in this passage. How has the story developed? What new information does it present? Are there any portions of the passage that don't make sense? Tell students that when they present their passage to the class, someone in another group might be able to answer their questions.

- Have students choose a spokesperson and a record-keeper to take notes on the group's discussion. The record-keeper is also responsible for handing in these notes, along with each group member's annotated passage. (I hardly ever glance at these sheets, but simply having something that must be turned in at the end of the period seems to help students stay on task for a substitute teacher.)

- During the next thirty minutes, have groups present what they have found in their passages to the class. The groups should proceed in chronological order so that these "expert" explanations foster a developing understanding of last night's reading.

- For the final five minutes of class, students turn over their annotated passage and write about how this excerpt relates to the larger work. What purpose does this paragraph serve in terms of advancing the story? How are characters developing? Have new problems been introduced?

- Before the bell rings, make sure students have copied down their homework reading assignment.

Substitute teachers need no more knowledge of literature to run this lesson plan than they do to turn on the VCR. All that is required is classroom management skills.

The Play's the Thing

I can already hear the arguments: "But what about Shakespeare, Shaw, Miller? Aren't plays meant to be seen, not read? Don't professional actors bring to life, through gesture and intonation, lines that would remain forever obscure to the teenage reader? Don't costumes and sets scaffold students' understanding of the action?" Yes. As a genre, plays can be one of the most difficult texts for students to read. And very few teenagers have ever seen a live professional performance. Thus, showing films like Kenneth Branaugh's *Henry V* and Franco Zeffirelli's *Romeo and Juliet* is a very good use of class time.

I first saw Marlon Brando as Antony when I was a sophomore in high school. After a hiatus of six years, I have seen the 1953 Joseph Mankiewicz version of *Julius Caesar* every year since, easily twenty-five times, and that doesn't count the years when I taught two periods of tenth-grade English and would view the movie twice in one day. James Mason as Brutus still gives me goose bumps when he tells Cassius that Portia is dead. Great actors make a play come alive.

What teachers need to be on guard for, however, is structuring students' viewing of a film in such a way that it actually discourages them from reading the text. I often use short excerpts from the movie or an audiotape as we begin a play in order to help students hear Shakespeare's language in their heads as they read. I also like showing students alternative versions of the same speech, for example Hamlet's "To be or not to be" soliloquy. Many video stores have at least three versions of *Hamlet* to compare. But when students know the teacher will show them a film clip of last night's reading assignment or the whole film before they have to write their papers, I find that they don't push themselves as hard as they might to unlock the text on the page. By all means let students see Shakespeare in performance, but also make sure they learn to negotiate his written words.

Novels Are Another Story

Novels are another story. Film adaptations of novels, even the Sergei Bondarchuk *War and Peace* that runs for 507 minutes, have been so abbreviated that even the best of them are seriously flawed. It is simply not possible to compress 300 to 600 pages into 90 minutes. For comparison, screenplays (which are double-spaced and have very wide margins) typically run fewer than 200 pages. Don't we hate it when students turn to Cliffs Notes or the Electronic Library for plot summaries instead of reading the book we have assigned? Don't we practically accuse them of cheating, particularly of cheating themselves? Why then should we encourage students to watch film versions of classics? Movies, even powerful productions, can only ever hope to skim the surface of a great book.

For example, the 1946 version of *Great Expectations* is considered by many as one of the greatest films ever made. As such, viewing this movie would seem the ideal solution for slow or reluctant readers who, if they could be persuaded to persevere, might well need six weeks to complete Dickens' (1864) four-hundred-page novel. But as wonderful as Oscar Award–winning cinematographer Guy

---

Green's graveyard scene is, these students would be much the poorer for never having constructed the following scene for themselves:

> "Hold your noise!" cried a terrible voice, as a man started up from among the graves at the side of the church porch. "Keep still, you little devil, or I'll cut your throat!"
>
> A fearful man, all in coarse grey, with a great iron on his leg. A man with no hat, and with broken shoes, and with an old rag tied round his head. A man who had been soaked in water, and smothered in mud, and lamed by stones, and cut by flints, and stung by nettles, and torn by briars; who limped and shivered, and glared and growled; and whose teeth chattered in his head as he seized me by the chin.
>
> "O! Don't cut my throat, sir," I pleaded in terror. "Pray don't do it, sir."
>
> "Tell us your name!" said the man. "Quick!"
>
> "Pip, sir." (1–2)

This is powerful prose, rich in detail and full of passion. To offer students a film version in place of Dickens' sentences seems a poor substitute. Teenagers will take the substitute, of course. But though they will come away with the gist of the story, they won't have learned how to read a Dickens novel. Most will tell you they don't care, but how could they care when they have no idea what they are missing? High-quality film adaptations have a place in the curriculum, but only after the novel has been read and students' reading assessed.

Viewing Films Outside of Class

One way to make room for the viewing of important films like *The Grapes of Wrath* and *Great Expectations* within the curriculum is to show them during students' lunch period or after school. What I like about this method is that it often allows me to interact with students who struggled with the reading and now find that the film has helped them make sense of what was opaque to them in the text. I offer these students the opportunity to rewrite their papers on the novel. My goal was never to catch them out in their reading, but to help them construct a powerful understanding of the book. If the film allowed this to happen, they should have the chance to demonstrate what they now know.

Another way that I have integrated film into the curriculum without eating into class time is to assign students viewing homework. Asking students to group themselves with others who live nearby because they are going to be watching a video together, I assign each group a paired book and film. In these pairings I have looked for films that do not faithfully re-create what a writer has done but that provide rather interesting and successful adaptations of the writer's ideas. For example:

1. *Emma* and *Clueless*

2. *One Flew Over the Cuckoo's Nest*

3. *The Color Purple*

4. *Do Androids Dream of Electric Sheep* (by Philip K. Dick) and *Blade Runner*

5. *The Joy Luck Club*

6. *Dr. Jekyll and Mr. Hyde* and *Mary Reilly* (This is the classic story retold from the point of view of Dr. Jekyll's housekeeper. The film was made from a book by Valerie Martin also called *Mary Reilly*.)

What is particularly interesting about *The Color Purple* and *The Joy Luck Club* pairings is that in both cases the authors were intimately involved with the making of the films. I have to be very careful about getting signed parent permission for students to view any R-rated film. I also find the assignment works best if I own copies of the videotapes that I can lend to students. At $12 to $13 each, this hasn't been a big investment. Our public library also has a huge collection of films on video that they rent out at the rate of $1 a film for five nights.

Once they have read the book and seen the movie, students write a comparison/contrast essay about the two experiences. One of the things I like best about this assignment is the way students find it quite natural to help one another develop ideas for their papers. Often less able readers see things in the film that their peers have missed. More able writers help these students organize what they have seen into coherent form. Viewing the film together outside school time seems to help build community in the classroom.

The goal of this assignment is to help students realize for themselves that any film is an interpretation. Experienced readers viewing *The Age of Innocence* hold their own memory and interpretation of the novel up against Martin Scorsese's for comparison. Student viewers rarely have this confidence. They often accept the filmmaker's version at face value and assume their own reading must have been somehow mistaken. How could Scorsese be wrong? Unsure of their newly formed interpretations, students abandon their own reading and assume the filmmaker's as valid and authoritative. Talented though she may be, Michelle Pfeiffer is no Madame Olenska to my reader's eye.

I want students to leave class with Edith Wharton's description of Madam Olenska's looks rather than with the interpretation of Pfeiffer's makeup artist and costume designer. Newland remembers Madam Olenska's appearance after returning from Europe:

> She came rather late, one hand still ungloved, and fastening a bracelet about her wrist; yet she entered without any appearance of haste of embarrassment the drawing-room in which New York's most chosen company was somewhat awfully assembled. In the middle of the room she paused, looking about her with a grave mouth and smiling eyes; and in that instant Newland Archer re-

jected the general verdict on her looks. It was true that her early radiance was gone. The red cheeks had paled; she was thin, worn, a little older-looking than her age, which must have been nearly thirty. But there was about her the mysterious authority of beauty, a sureness in the carriage of the head, the movement of the eyes, which, without being in the least theatrical, struck his as highly trained and full of a conscious power. . . . It frightened him to think what had gone into the making of her eyes. (60–62)

How can a scene in a movie, even an excellent movie, begin to capture the subtlety of the world Wharton re-creates in this passage. How sad to offer students substitutes when the real thing is there for the reading.

Almost every classic has been considered at one time or another for production by a filmmaker. This is for good reason. Classic stories have—among other things—unforgettable characters, a riveting plot line, and an enduring message. It is a recipe for success on the big screen as well as on the small page. But books and film are two very different media and I don't believe they mix well in an English classroom. By all means, encourage your students to enroll in a film class, but when they are with us, it's best to keep them reading.

CHAPTER NINE

Readers with Roots and Wings

For many the mere mention of Matthew Arnold's name suggests elitism and the worship of literary masterpieces. But what is often omitted from this shorthand version of the man is that Matthew Arnold was an educational reformist who urged the English to compare their school system with those in other countries. He believed that a radical rethinking of teaching practices was needed, and that the place to start was with self-criticism.

In the preface to *Culture and Anarchy,* Arnold (1932) explains that his purpose for writing the book was

> to recommend culture as the great help out of our present diffi-
> culties; culture being a pursuit of our total perfection by means
> of getting to know, on all the matters which most concern us, the
> best which has been thought and said in the world; and through
> this knowledge, turning a stream of fresh and free thought upon
> our stock notions and habits. (6)

I have tried in the preceding chapters to offer ways for making the best that has been written accessible to contemporary readers. Like Arnold I feel we have gotten ourselves into some "present difficulties." For too many students, the middle and high school English curriculum has been so watered down that students no longer get to know "the best of which has been thought and said in the world." This is a terrible shame, particularly with incidents of teenage violence and despair on the rise. Many children today are virtually raising themselves. In some cases immigrant parents must work several jobs simply to keep food on the table. In other households both parents are high-powered professionals with workdays of twelve or more hours. Young people are spending long unsupervised hours in front of television and online. Unfortunately neither of these sites are good sources of the best of what has been thought and said in the world. Teachers, and especially English teachers, may be students' primary access to such information. Classical literature is not the only place where young people can learn about the best of what has been thought, but it is one place.

Identifying with Characters

To those who say that contemporary teens can't relate to the characters in classical literature, I would suggest rereading Chapter VI of *Great Expectations.* The convict Magwitch has just confessed to the "crime" Pip committed by stealing food and drink from Pip's sister's house. Though Pip is relieved, he is also troubled by this first experience of his own duplicity:

> My state of mind regarding the pilfering from which I had been so unexpectedly exonerated, did not impel me to frank disclosure; but I hope it had some dregs of good at the bottom of it. I do not recall that I felt any tenderness of conscience in reference to Mrs. Joe, when the fear of being found out was lifted off me. But I loved Joe—perhaps for no better reason in those early days than because the dear fellow let me love him—and, as to him, my inner self was not so easily composed. It was much upon my mind (particularly when I first saw him looking about for his file) that I ought to tell Joe the whole truth. Yet I did not, and for

the reason that I mistrusted that if I did, he would think me worse than I was. (37)

What teenager, which of us, has not known such a moment? Most of us want to be good and tell the truth as we have been taught to do, but then circumstances complicate matters. Decisions in real life, or in good literature, seldom appear in black or white. As we learn with Pip how to negotiate this gray area, we experience a fall from grace. Some call this growing up. Much of the skill in bringing classical literature to life for students is a matter of helping them see themselves in Pip and other protagonists.

In *The Gutenberg Elegies, The Fate of Reading in an Electronic Age,* Sven Birkerts (1994) writes about how "adolescence is the ideal laboratory for the study of reading and self-formation" (89):

> How does reading work on the psyche during what is surely its most volatile period of change? There is no pinning it down, naturally, but we might begin with the most obvious sort of answer: the role of specific books and characters. We get reports of this influence all the time in interviews and memoirs. The subject tells of living with Tom Sawyer or David Copperfield or Elizabeth Bennet. There follows the desire to do what Tom did, to be like young Elizabeth. These recognitions are eventually externalized as ideas and in that form guide the behavior along after the spell of the reading passes. I vividly remember situations in which I acted in a certain way—more bravely, more recklessly—because I believed that that was what Jack London would have done. (89–90)

I am not ashamed of my desire to shape my students' behavior. I think there are some ways of conducting oneself that are preferable to others. The best I can do is offer them stories where characters behave in ways that, in Matthew Arnold's words, allow them to turn

---

"a stream of fresh and free thought" upon their "stock notions and habits."

The challenge for teachers is to make the self-formation that Sven Birkerts describes occur for students who loathe reading. It often seems to me that an invisible barrier exists between the book and the student. Most of the time, these students can read but won't. And the longer they persist in this refusal, the more their reading skills deteriorate from lack of use. Like a leg in a cast, reading muscles atrophy.

I don't need standardized test scores to identify such students. After just a few days in class they identify themselves. Signs to look for include a reluctance to carry any book at all (I may have just handed out copies of a text and already the student asks if he can store it in the classroom), a shrug of the shoulders when we go around the class describing our summer reading, and a desire to sit as far as possible from me.

What I don't want to happen with such a student is that before I have had a chance to change her mind about the book we are reading, she should feel like a failure for not completing an assignment. Once a pattern of bad marks is established, I have probably lost her. I make it a point to look directly at this student when setting the stage for what we are about to read. It's not only a matter of making sure she is paying attention but also a matter of letting her know her understanding matters to me. Obviously when there are ten students in the class who all need such eye contact, the challenge is enormous.

When I have a whole class of reluctant readers, I scaffold their reading in ways that at first may seem authoritative and overly structured, but my hope is that as the year progresses I will be able to disassemble the scaffolding. For example:

- When students arrive, the day's lesson with book title, author, page numbers, and a summary of activities is written clearly on the board for them to see.

- I check that everyone has a book in hand (and keep a few extras in my desk for those who don't, reminding them that they need to bring their book every day).

- I may ask students to scan what they read last night for a passage that struck them for some reason or another. Handing out Post-it notes, I have students mark this spot and then copy this sentence or paragraph in their journals.

- I then have students exchange journals and ask them to read what their partner has written and write four or five sentences explaining what this passage says to them.

- Once journals have been returned to their owners, we begin a classroom discussion using what others have said about the quotations they chose as a springboard. I am able to call on anyone because even if the student is reluctant to speak out in class, he can always read what his partner wrote.

On a good day this activity can lead us to a thorough discussion of the chapter under scrutiny. I have to work very hard not to dominate the conversation. The best check I've found of whether or not I am is to note whether I have said something between each student response. If I want students to talk to one another, I need to practice restraint.

Five minutes before the period ends I try to help students anticipate stumbling blocks in the pages that have been assigned for homework. I have them turn to places where there is a break in the text and explain if there is a change of time, place, or speaker indicated by the break. I warn them if this section of the story is going to include a lot of description or a lot of dialogue in dialect. I hand out extra Post-it notes and urge them to use them as they read to indicate any places where they have questions.

Over the past twenty years the National Writing Project has taught most of us in English classrooms that assigning writing is not the same thing as teaching writing. We now need to discover the similar truth about assigning reading and teaching reading.

Playing chauffeur to a station wagon full of tenth-grade boys, I eavesdropped on their conversation about compulsory military service. After several minutes of debating whether girls should be drafted, the subject shifted to war. They had all recently read *All Quiet on the Western Front*:

Ramsey: Look at what happened to Paul. His teacher and every-body in the town had him all hyped up about being a soldier and then Bam! He's in the middle of hell.

Peter: Paul didn't have a clue what he was getting himself into when he signed up. They fed him a bunch of lies about honor and glory and the Fatherland. If there was a war and I got drafted, I wouldn't go.

James: Not even if your mom said you should?

Peter: Mothers don't know anything. Paul's mom still didn't get it even when Paul came back on leave all messed up in his head. She thought he looked good in his uniform.

Ramsey: I don't believe you, Peter. You're Jewish. You wouldn't have fought Hitler?

Peter: O.K. I'd fight Hitler but that's different.

James: I think it's always different. And I think guys like Paul always get screwed in war. It was a good book, though, Mrs. Jago. And, hey, thanks for the ride.

As the boys piled out of the car, they had no idea how happy they had just made me. *All Quiet on the Western Front*: a book they had read at my behest, caused them to turn a stream of fresh and free thought onto their own stock ideas about military service and war.

———

Learning from Characters Who Are Unlike Us

Stories that cause students to reflect in this manner are not always stories in which the characters look like them. Sometimes it is easier to learn from a character who appears to have nothing whatsoever in common with us, at least on the surface.

When I was nine an aunt who knew I loved to read gave me a box of books. The children's hospital where she worked was discarding Annie Fellows Johnston's *The Little Colonel* series, and she hated to see them go to waste. The books were written around 1900 and are set in what remained of plantation life following the Civil War. The main character is a headstrong little girl nicknamed the Little Colonel after her Confederate hero grandfather. I adored reading about this little girl's exploits and outbursts. I reveled in her boldness. The Little Colonel, brash and outspoken, embodied everything I, whiny and bookish, was not.

Unfortunately Volume 3 of the twelve-volume set, *The Little Colonel's House Party*, was missing. I devoured the eleven I had and for years dreamed of the wonderful things that must have happened at that party. I knew the missing volume must be the best book in the world. A few months ago I amused my students by showing them a worn volume and telling them that I had been waiting thirty-five years to read this book. They were open-mouthed when I told them I had paid $68 for this tired-looking copy of Annie Fellows Johnston's *The Little Colonel's House Party*, but they could see my eyes shining in anticipation of turning its pages.

What I discovered as I read was more curious than any children's party. Politically incorrect in any number of ways, the book stands as a charming period piece. Characters behave decently toward one another. The Little Colonel may be willful and spoiled, but she is genuinely contrite when her haughtiness hurts others or when she learns how self-absorption has blinded her to others less fortunate than herself. These are issues that I have had to struggle with in my own character all my life. How strange that I should have somehow known even as a child that this would be the case. The Little Colonel provided me with a remarkable model for behavior even though the circumstances of her life could not have been more different from my own. Self-improvement is the last thing on the mind of a child, yet for avid readers, it always seems that the books we need find us.

Challenging Children's Literature

Another thing that interested me about Johnston's book was the complexity of its vocabulary and sentence structure. Writing for young children's amusement, Johnston employed complex sentences like these:

> Under the blossoms rode the Little Colonel, all in white herself this May morning, except the little Napoleon hat of black velvet, set jauntily over her short light hair. Into the cockade she had stuck a spray of locust blossoms, and as she rode slowly along she fastened a bunch of them behind each ear of her pony, whose coat was as soft and black as the velvet of her hat. (1921, 13)

I imagine this sentence would rate quite high in terms of its readability level or Lexile score, yet Annie Fellows Johnston's books were wildly popular among young readers in the 1920s and 1930s. I doubt that children were smarter then. I do think we underestimate the kind of sentences young readers can negotiate when the story is a compelling one. Here is another passage to compare against the kind of prose current textbooks find appropriate for fourth- or fifth-grade readers:

> The dust flew, dogs barked, and chickens ran squawking across the road out of the way. Heads were thrust out of the windows as

the two vanished up the dusty pike, and an old graybeard loafing in front of the corner grocery gave an amused chuckle. A little while later the three white envelopes were jogging sociably along, side by side in a mail-bag, on their way to Louisville. But their course did not lie together long. In the city post-office they separated, and sent on their different ways, like three white carrier-pigeons, to bid the guests make ready for the Little Colonel's house party. (24)

Johnston used semicolons frequently and employed a level of vocabulary that would challenge many of my ninth graders. On a single page I found the following words: *eccentric, imposing, picturesque, imperious.*

Johnston also incorporated dialect into her text and simply assumed that her young readers would figure out what the odd-looking words meant.

"Oh, deah," croaked the Little Colonel like a dismal raven, as she waited at the head of the stairs for the girls to finish dressing. "This is the la-st mawnin' we'll all go racin' down to breakfast togethah! I'm glad that Betty isn't goin' away for a while longah. If you all had to leave a the same time, it would be so lonesome that I couldn't stand it." (248)

A child who grows up reading children's literature that invites the reader to hear language as spoken will have little difficulty in high school with the dialect in *Great Expectations, Huckleberry Finn, Their Eyes Were Watching God,* or *The Color Purple.* One of the reasons teachers sometimes give up on teaching the classics is that these books pose too many textual challenges for students all at once. Sensitive to their students' discomfort, teachers choose simpler novels. For some students their lack of preparation is a result of their own aversion to reading. For others it may be a result of reading books that didn't stretch them. While we have made significant progress in terms of eradicating stereotypes in children's literature, we may have gone backwards in terms of rich language and complex syntax.

Sandra Stotsky, the author of *Losing Our Language,* contends that in response to demands for wider representation and easier-to-read texts in elementary school readers, publishers have eliminated much of the literature that once prepared students for the challenging academic and literary texts they face in high school and college. She sees vocabulary development as the key:

> Children's language development is the engine that drives intellectual growth, and the language of schooling is the engine that drives academic achievement. Thought and language interact at the level of the word. (1999, 13)

The literature we offer children, and particularly the literature we teach in school, should be both culturally diverse and stylistically complex. There's no reason for either/or. Examples of contemporary classics that belong in the high school curriculum for their outstanding literary merit include Lesley Marmon Silko's *Ceremony,* Toni Morrison's *Beloved,* August Wilson's plays, Louise Erdrich's *Love Medicine,* Gabriel García Márquez's short stories, Maxine Hong Kingston's *Woman Warrior,* and many others. Every one of these texts offers readers the kind of enduring stories and rich language that defines a classic.

Stotsky's argument brings us to the issue of classical versus multicultural literature (we had to get to it sometime). Mark Twain or Toni Morrison? William Shakespeare or Athol Fugard? Ernest Hemingway or Leslie Silko? Teachers need not fret over what must be taken out of the curriculum if a new work is included. The solution is obvious. Students must simply read more books. Of course, as Harold Bloom (1994) points out, "Who reads must choose, since there is literally not enough time to read everything even if one does nothing but read" (15). But most students could easily read twice as many books as they do now merely by using the hours they waste staring into a television or computer screen. Of course persuading students to pull themselves away from those seductive machines is extremely difficult. Teachers are going to need all the help they can get from parents.

The California Reading/Language Arts Standards (1999) call for twelfth-grade students to be reading two million words a year or about twenty-five books. Even the most contentious English departments should be able to agree upon a list of core readings when they can choose so many titles for students to read. Students could be given some choice here, too.

A Summer Reading Program

Last year at Santa Monica High School we experimented with having students recommend some of the summer reading titles. A group of ninth graders were irate over our selections and insisted that if they were going to be made to read over the summer they should at least have some say over what they read. These enterprising fourteen-year-olds surveyed the student body regarding their attitudes toward summer reading and presented their findings to the English Department. We compromised by selecting three books with similar themes and allowed students to choose the one that most appealed to them. Their second title for summer reading could be entirely of their own choosing.

We sent notice of this summer reading assignment home in a letter to parents describing the importance of reading along with a long list of titles students might choose to consider for their free-choice book. The books were organized under headings such as "The Boys' Water Polo Team Recommends," "Midnight Special Bookstore Recommends," "The Black Student Union Recommends," as well as more traditional groupings of thrillers and science fiction titles. I do not offer this summer reading program to you as a perfected product. We have been requiring summer reading for the past ten years and every spring decide to tinker with it a bit more. What we found this fall was that there seemed to be less resentment of the summer reading assignment when students had been involved in the process.

Competing Canons

Debates over what students should be reading have spread from academe into public discourse. In the spring of 1998 two San Francisco school board members proposed that more than half of the required high school books should be by nonwhite authors. Board members Steve Phillips and Keith Jackson said they wanted to ensure that reading lists reflected the makeup of their racially diverse city. At the time their proposal was made, San Francisco required only three books—*Canterbury Tales, Romeo and Juliet,* and *Huckleberry Finn*—and recommended that students read up to ten books annually from a broad selection of authors. No specific titles or authors were specified.

The proposal caused an uproar. Radio talk show switchboards lit up with listeners passionate on both sides of the issue. Right-wing talk show host Rush Limbaugh scoffed at the proposal as another example of multiculturalism run amok. To my mind the most thoughtful response came from Shelley Fisher Fishkin (1998), professor of American studies and English at the University of Texas at Austin. She argued in a *Los Angeles Times* article that

> A quota for nonwhite writers dishonors the writers it purports to champion and insults the students it is meant to help. A quota system for nonwhite authors projects the idea that authors who

happen to be nonwhite are being taught primarily because they are nonwhite, not because their books are worth reading and studying. A quota system implies that an author's ethnicity is the most important aspect of his or her book.

The implication that students can relate only to writers from their own ethnic groups also is inherently demeaning. The nonwhite writers whose books the quota system would champion are a case in point. Maxine Hong Kingston drew her inspiration in large part from Walt Whitman. And Toni Morrison, along with Ralph Ellison and David Bradley, learned a lot about writing from reading Mark Twain.

San Francisco's seven-member school board voted unanimously to adopt a resolution pledging that authors on required reading lists be diverse in terms of race, ethnicity, and sexual orientation, striking a compromise between backers of the quota plan and traditionalists demanding that the classics remain in place.

The biggest problem with the old San Francisco reading list was not that it was too white or too male, but that it was too short. I think it is reasonable to expect students to read fifteen to twenty books during the course of the school year and at least three more during the summer. I always assign a novel over winter and spring breaks and don't lose a moment of sleep over students who tell me they will be otherwise occupied. Taking a plane? That's a perfect time to read. Visiting relatives? Grandma will be proud to see you with a book. Working a job? What better way to relax when you get home than with Holden Caulfield.

Paired Texts

One idea for confronting the canon controversy is having students read more books. Another idea is to have them read paired texts. English departments inadvertently downplay the influence other voices have had upon the American character when they teach only classics. Another false message this kind of curriculum sends is that American literature ended with Hemingway. Teaching from an exclusively multicultural reading list, on the other hand, gives students the impression that these works sprang forth in full bloom, unrelated to and disconnected from the traditions and authors of the past. The classics are touchstones for much of the writing that has followed.

For example, Zora Neale Hurston's *Their Eyes Were Watching God* could be paired with Mark Twain's *The Adventures of Huckleberry Finn*. Janie, Hurston's heroine, sets out upon a journey of self-discovery much like Huck's, though as a black woman her challenges and consequent triumph look very different. Both novels employ dialect, but if teachers are willing to work through this obstacle with Twain, why not with Hurston?

Along with Nathaniel Hawthorne's *The Scarlet Letter*, I would teach Bharati Mukherjee's *Jasmine*. Like Hester Prynne, Mukherjee's main character, Jasmine, is marked as an outsider. But while Hester chooses to remain within the community that has branded her, Jasmine flees her traditional Hindu past for the brave new fields of Iowa. Both women find that they must reinvent themselves in order to survive. Hester stays within the Puritan world partly for her daughter, Pearl, while Jasmine carries her as-yet-unborn pearl off to California. Are these alternate solutions to similar problems a sign of the characters' times? Such interesting questions crop up often when students read across time periods.

Similarly, F. Scott Fitzgerald's classic *The Great Gatsby* could be paired with Jay McInerney's *Bright Lights, Big City*. Like Jay Gatsby, McInerney's narrator (who is never named in the story and refers to himself in the second person) is obsessed with the bright promise of life. And what life promises the bright young narrator in the clubs of New York in the 1980s looks remarkably like what the Jazz Age offered in the 1920s.

Jay Gatsby was fascinated by the earning and spending of money and, like the young businessmen of his time, was bitterly determined to be successful. He measured his success, failure, and even virtue in monetary terms. McInerney's hero is similarly fixated. With wit and controlled substances to sustain him, he too pursues the American dream. What better way to teach the literature of a period than to ask students to draw parallels between the periods, observing as they do the American character in transition.

Other pairings with rich thematic connections include:

- *A Doll's House* by Henrik Ibsen with *Top Girls* by Caryl Churchill

- *Hamlet* by William Shakespeare with *Rosencranz and Guildenstern Are Dead* by Tom Stoppard

- *Romeo and Juliet* by William Shakespeare with *Like Water for Chocolate* by Laura Esquivel

- *No Exit* by Jean-Paul Sartre with *Oleanna* by David Mamet

- *Jane Eyre* by Charlotte Brontë with *Annie John* by Jamaica Kincaid

- *My Antonia* by Willa Cather with *Krik? Krak!* by Edwidge Danticat

- *The Awakening* by Kate Chopin with *Mama Day* by Gloria Naylor

- *The Red Badge of Courage* by Stephen Crane with *The Things They Carried* by Tim O'Brien

- *Notes from the Underground* by Fyodor Dostoevsky with *Invisible Man* by Ralph Ellison

- *Sister Carrie* by Theodore Dreiser with *The Life and Loves of a She-Devil* by Fay Weldon

- *Madame Bovary* by Gustave Flaubert with *Flaubert's Parrot* by Julian Barnes

---

- *Daisy Miller* by Henry James with *Breakfast at Tiffany's* by Truman Capote

- *Cannery Row* by John Steinbeck with *All Stories Are True* by John Edgar Wideman

- *The Red Pony* by John Steinbeck with *All the Pretty Horses* by Cormac McCarthy

- *Dr. Jekyll and Mr. Hyde* by Robert Louis Stevenson with *Dr. Haggard's Disease* by Patrick McGrath

- *Fathers and Sons* by Ivan Turgenev with *Dreaming in Cuban* by Cristina Garcia

- *The Age of Innocence* by Edith Wharton with *July's People* by Nadine Gordimer

- *The Picture of Dorian Gray* by Oscar Wilde with *Paris Trout* by Pete Dexter

- *All Quiet on the Western Front* by Erich Maria Remarque with *Birdsong* by Sebastian Faulks

Teachers as Readers

One problem with pairing classical and contemporary texts is that few teachers born before 1970 studied writers like Hurston, Mukherjee, or McInerney in college. As a result, we are often unsure about which texts to choose for critical pairings. But teachers need to be pioneers on the frontiers of our field. For those of us in a position to choose books and design curriculum, that means reading.

I am often asked how I find time to read. I have no answer. I always carry a book with me and steal a few reading minutes while waiting to pick up my son from soccer practice or sometimes from the sidelines while others watch the midfield action. I think we should take our reading as seriously as we take their health. We find time for exercise and regular check-ups. We dutifully count fat content and calories. I would like to suggest that we pay equal attention to our literary diet. We owe it to ourselves and to our students to take better care of ourselves as readers.

One of the best ways to make time for one's own reading is to join a book group. Having to finish a book for the next meeting helps me say, "Sorry, I have to finish my book" when others make demands on my time. The pleasure of talking about books with adults (and the guilt I feel if I still have fifty pages left) is a wonderful incentive to make the group's deadline.

Keeping my own love for books and for talking about books active and alive helps me be a better literature teacher. The more honestly I model the habits of mind of a lifelong reader, the more likely students are to follow my lead. Teenagers spot a phony a mile away.

Denby's Adventures with the Classics

At the age of forty-eight, David Denby (1996), film critic for *New York* magazine, did what so many teachers who are readers dream of doing—he went back to school. Vaguely dissatisfied with life and frustrated by the arid debate over the canon that was raging at the time, Denby returned to Columbia University and enrolled in the two required courses in classical literature that he had taken in 1961 as a freshman. Denby explains why:

> . . . in part because I no longer knew what I knew. I felt that what I had read or understood was slipping away. I possessed information without knowledge, opinions without principles, instincts without beliefs. The foundations of the building were turning to sand while I sat in the upper balconies looking out at the sea. . . . Reading 'the great books' may seem an odd solution to a midlife crisis or a crisis of identity or whatever it was. Why not travel or hunt elephants? Chase teenage girls? Live in a monastery? These, I believe, are the traditional methods—for men, at least—of

dealing with such problems. But if I wanted adventure, I wanted it in a way that made sense for me. Reading seriously, I thought, might be one way of ending my absorption in media life, a way of finding the edges again. (15–16)

Denby also wanted to see how others were reading, to see how contemporary students, weaned on movies and television, responded to the "great books." So for a year he sat side by side with Columbia students reading Homer, Sapho, Plato, Sophocles, Aristotle, Aeschylus, Euripides, Virgil, the Old Testament, the New Testament, Augustine, Machiavelli, Hobbes, Lock, Dante, Boccaccio, Hume, Kant, Montaigne, Rousseau, Shakespeare, Hegel, Austen, Marx, Mill, Nietzche, Beauvoir, Conrad, and Woolf, all the while keeping a journal.

The first book on the Columbia reading list was *The Iliad.* Though Denby has a far richer working vocabulary than ninth graders have at their disposal, his experience with the first pages of the epic resembles theirs to a remarkable degree:

> Reading the poem in its entirety is like fronting a storm that refuses to slacken or die. At first, I had to fight my way through it; I wasn't bored but I was rebellious, my attention a bucking horse unwilling to submit to the harness. It was too long, I thought, too brutal and repetitive and, for all its power as a portrait of war, strangely distant from us. . . . Movie-fed, I wasn't used to working so hard, and as I sat on my sofa at home, reading, my body, in daydreams, kept leaping away from the seat and into the bedroom, where I would sink into bed and turn on the TV, or to the kitchen, where I would open the fridge. (34–35)

Entering a Fictional World

Just as it takes students days, sometimes weeks, to settle in to an epic or novel, so it took Denby time to adapt to the demands classical literature puts upon a reader. The problem of entry is a challenge for all readers, and breaking in to a new book is never easy. I warn students that this is the case and demonstrate how I begin reading a book. Vygotsky (1962) describes learning as a process by which children "grow into the intellectual life around them" (88). If I want students to grow to be sophisticated readers, I need to nurture their developing skills with challenging texts. The more effectively I am able to model how an expert reader settles into a book, the more likely their movie-fed selves will be able to get into the reading.

I tell students that when I pick up a new book I sometimes read the first few sentences over and over. This is not only to make sure I haven't missed an important detail, but more important to help me become used to the rise and fall of the writer's language. I need to find the author's rhythm and to match my own inner ear to that sound.

I also describe to students how within a very few paragraphs I must re-create the story's setting in my head. If I read that snow is swirling about a man's legs as he crosses an empty airfield, I picture that image. Reading on, the image develops. Is it day or night? Is there a moon? Re-creating the story's setting is essential because it will be the backdrop for everything that follows. Readers don't need to remind themselves continually of the setting any more than we need to remind ourselves as we sit in the classroom that the school is located in Santa Monica, California. But we do need to see the fictional world with our mind's eye.

With students who struggle with visualizing the printed word, it sometimes helps to have them read a descriptive passage from early in the novel and ask them to sketch the scene. Assure them that artistic skill is not required here but that they should try to draw what the author has described. When students do this in groups, those who have never imagined that words actually create pictures see for themselves how others make this happen.

Ornery and Difficult Books

In his epilogue to *Great Books,* Denby tackles the sticky issue of the relevance of great books to contemporary students' lives:

> By the end of my year in school, I knew that the culture-ideologues, both left and right, are largely talking nonsense. Both groups simplify and caricature the Western tradition. They ignore its ornery and difficult books; they ignore its actual students, most of whom have been dispossessed. Whether white, black, Asian, or Latino, American students rarely arrive at college as habitual readers, which means that few of them have more than a nominal connection to the past. It is absurd to speak, as does the academic left, of classic Western texts dominating and silencing everyone but a ruling elite of white males. The vast majority of white students do not know the intellectual tradition that is allegedly theirs any better than black or brown ones do. They have not read its books, and when they do read them, they may respond well, but they will not respond in the way that the academic left supposes. For there is only one "hegemonic discourse" in the lives of American undergraduates, and that is the mass media. Most high schools can't begin to compete against a torrent of imagery and sound that makes every moment but the present seem quaint, bloodless, or dead. (459)

I will never stop trying to compete with those images, that racket. While I don't believe that it would be the end of civilization as we know it were we to stop teaching the ornery and difficult classics, I do think it would be a terrible mistake. Great books offer readers a range of ideas, a range of pleasures, unavailable elsewhere. By taking us into strange landscapes and showing us from the inside out how other people think and feel, the classics "civilize" us.

The classics also teach us about ourselves. I used to think of reading as an escape. Anyone's life was more interesting than mine. But the more I read, the more I found myself inside those books. For the duration of the novel, I became Elizabeth Bennet in *Pride and Prejudice* and Holden Caulfield in *Catcher in the Rye* and saw things in their character, some good, some not-so-good, that were inside me, too. There was no escape.

Teachers as Characters

One of the oddest things about being a teacher is that you can sometimes find yourself a character in the stories students tell. I know that the day Christina fainted in my arms has passed into Santa Monica High School folklore. The class was talking about John Gardner's novel *Grendel,* and someone was using a particularly gruesome passage as evidence for a point he was making. As the monster began to tear the queen apart, Christina, pale and wan, walked to the front of the room. In my ear she whispered, "Mrs. Jago, can I please go to the   " At which point she collapsed. Lifting her head from the carpet I turned to the class and remarked, "Ah, the power of literature."

How this story has been told and retold over the years, I shudder to think. My guess is that the part where I call the nurse and Christina is diagnosed with a bad case of missing breakfast is somehow omitted. Students tell the story to make a point. Mrs. Jago is crazy about literature.

Just last week, Lena, an eleventh grader, accosted me at the end of class. "Mrs. Jago, somebody said you once dated a poet. Is this true?"

Not having the foggiest notion where this question had come from, let alone where it was going, I decided to buy time. "I don't understand what you mean by *dated,* Lena."

"Oh, you know, went out with."

"No, I don't think so, but I did once kiss Walter Mosley."

Lotus Thompson, just on her way out, stopped dead in her tracks. "You kissed Walter Mosley?"

"It was at a convention, and I had just said something nice about *Devil in a Blue Dress*, and, well, there were about a hundred other people in the room."

Lena and Lotus looked meaningfully at one another and departed, concocting who knows what story about their teacher who is obsessed with books. I hope it's a good one.

CHAPTER 10

Book Lists of Classics, an Eclectic Collection

However authoritative a book list pretends to be, most are actually quite arbitrary. Lists include and exclude texts based upon criteria that are sometimes transparent even to the list makers. When the Modern Library released its list of the hundred best novels written in English in the twentieth century, it was met with outrage. How could James Dickey's *Deliverance* be better than anything Joseph Conrad ever wrote? How is it possible that not a single book by Doris Lessing, Nadine Gordimer, Patrick White, Toni Morrison, or John Updike appears? Is *Ulysses* really the best book written in the twentieth century?

"So make your own list," said the publishers of the Modern Library, and they proceeded to provide a Web site where readers could create alternative lists. I like that response. Readers enjoy making lists of "best" books almost as much as they like poking holes in other people's lists.

James Strickland (1997), English professor at Slippery Rock University, Pennsylvania, offers his take on the nature of book lists:

> Nick Hornby's characters in *High Fidelity* are constantly play-
> ing a game that involves picking the top five something: top

five sub-titled films: *Betty Blue, Subway, Tie Me Up! Tie me Down!, the Vanishing, Diva* . . . top five favorite recording artists: madness, Eurythmics, Bob Dylan, Joni Mitchell, Bob Marley . . . top five side one track ones (mine: Janie Jones, the Clash from *The Clash* . . .). The reason that his characters can play that game, and we can by extension, is that the items on the list are debatable. If there were agreement about the all-time top five Dylan songs, ther'd be no point making a list. The fun is in offering a different set of selections. If each of us made a list of the top five works to read in 10th grade, there would be some agreement, but each of the items would probably be worthy of inclusion. The inclusively compromising among us might suggest combining the lists to make a top twenty-five works for 10th grade. But what of the 26th book? And the 27th? Any mathematician will tell you there is no last number—there's always one more to add (n+1). (17)

The lists that follow make no claim to authority. They are the personal choices of one reader: me. I got the idea from a monograph by Anna Quindlen (1998), *How Reading Changed My Life.* In it, Quindlen describes her own life as a child reader. She explains how the habits she acquired have stayed with her to this day. Her extended essay is a testimonial to reading.

> By the time I became an adult, I realized that while my satisfaction in the sheer act of reading had not abated in the least, the world was often as hostile, or at least as blind, to the joy as had been my girlfriends banging on our screen door, begging me to put down the book—"that stupid book," they usually called it, no matter what book it happened to be. While we pay lip service to the virtues of reading, the truth is that there is still in our culture something that suspects those who read too much, whatever reading too much means, of being lazy, aimless dreamers, people who need to grow up and come outside where real life is. (9)

Avid readers often face such unspoken criticism, and it may be part of the reason many of my ninth-grade students, particularly boys, are so reluctant to be seen with a book in their hands. Most students do not look up to the readers in their midst. Readers are considered nerds or strivers. A few popular kids are secret readers, but like the secret writers who gravitate to fringe groups such as the school's creative writing magazine or underground newspaper staff, they mostly keep their passion for books to themselves. Within teenage culture, being a reader carries little status.

For that reason, I don't waste my breath trying to persuade reluctant readers that books are "cool." Instead I try to find the one particular book that just might hook one particular student. For Yesenia, a ninth grader who boasted that she had never finished a book in her life, it was a paperback biography of Tejana singer Selena. For tough-talking Andre it was Luis Rodriguez's *Always Running, La Vida Loca: Gang Days in L.A.* In class, I draw comparisons between these stories and their contemporary heroes with the classical stories and heroes we are studying. How was Selena's conviction about her talent similar to Beowulf's conviction regarding his own strength? How were the troubles Luis Rodriguez faced on the streets like Odysseus's? Can you see any similarities between how Luis dealt with sniffing glue and how Odysseus behaved in the Land of the Lotus Eaters?

Working with students like Yesenia and Andre over the course of a school year, I think I can begin to influence their reading habits. Last spring I showed their ninth-grade class this passage from Anna Quindlen's first chapter:

> In books I have traveled, not only to other worlds, but into my own. I learned who I was and who I wanted to be, what I might aspire to, and what I might dare to dream about my world and myself. More powerfully and persuasively than from the 'shalt nots' of the Ten Commandments, I learned the difference between good

and evil, right and wrong. One of my favorite childhood books, *A Wrinkle in Time,* described that evil, that wrong, existing in a different dimension from our own. But I felt that I, too, existed much of the time in a different dimension from everyone else I knew. There was waking, and there was sleeping. And then there were books, a kind of parallel universe in which anything might happen and frequently did, a universe in which I might be a new-comer but was never really a stranger. (6)

I asked students first to write and then to talk about what they thought of Quindlen's observations. Had a book ever made them feel like this?

Carlos: I kinda felt like that when I read *Always Running.* Andre said it was good so I looked at it and, yeah, it made me think about my neighborhood and how Luis almost really messed up his life with dope. I guess it gave me some ideas about good and bad.

Andre: Everybody knows drugs mess you up. What I liked about that story was the way Luis shows how even though you know they are bad news, most kids still use them. I'm always gonna remember that scene where he's sitting in the dried up L.A. River basin and almost dies.

Me: Why?

Andre: Luis has this like out-of-body experience like he's already dead but then he comes back. It's scary.

Me: What about books you have read that were set in places that are nothing like L.A. or people that you'll never meet?

Diana: You mean like Wealthow in *Beowulf?* What a stupid name. I kept thinking how she should never have married that old king. I mean she has this great hair, and I know she was saving her people and all that but I would never have done it. He's too old. Those scenes in their bedroom gave me the creeps. [Diana is

---

conflating plot details from John Gardner's *Grendel* with details from *Beowulf*.]

Carlos: She was a looker.

Me: Anna Quindlen talks about learning about good and evil from books. Did any of the things we read make you feel this way?

Diana: Not really. Well maybe in *Romeo and Juliet*. It shows how feuds and stuff are dumb, 'cause no one really wins. I guess I learned that but I know lots of people who would do just like Romeo if their best friend got killed in the streets.

It seems to me that at least within the context of the classroom, these students no longer found it a "nerdy" thing to be talking about books. The next challenge for me as their teacher would be to help them find their way to new books on their own. Anna Quindlen's whimsical lists of titles gave me an idea. Hers included *10 Mystery Novels I'd Most Like to Find in a Summer Rental*, *10 Books I Would Save in a Fire (If I Could Save Only 10)*, and my very favorite, *10 Books That Will Help a Teenager Feel More Human*. I wondered if I could come up with short lists that students might find as intriguing as I found Quindlen's.

I offer these lists from which to seed your own thinking about books. They were enormous fun to compile. At your next English department meeting, why not pass around headings of your own devising—*10 Classics for Teachers on the Verge of a Nervous Breakdown*, *10 Classics for Students Who Only Like Animal Stories*, *10 Science Fiction Classics*—and see what titles emerge. I have no doubt you will enjoy the exercise as much as I have.

10 Short Classics for Readers Short on Time

Winesburg, Ohio by Sherwood Anderson
Lady Susan by Jane Austen
The Stranger by Albert Camus

The Red Badge of Courage by Stephen Crane
Hard Times by Charles Dickens
The Ballad of the Sad Café by Carson McCullers
1984 by George Orwell
One Day in the Life of Ivan Denisovich by Alexander Solzhenitsyn
Of Mice and Men by John Steinbeck
Fathers and Sons, Ivan Turgenev

10 Classics in Their Own Time

Democracy by Joan Didion
Burger's Daughter by Nadine Gordimer
The Remains of the Day by Kazuo Ishiguro
The Woman Warrior by Maxine Hong Kingston
One Hundred Years of Solitude by Gabriel García Márquez
All the Pretty Horses by Cormac McCarthy
Beloved by Toni Morrison
The Things They Carried by Tim O'Brien
The English Patient by Michael Ondaatje
Midnight's Children by Salman Rushdie

10 Nonfiction Classics

Notes of a Native Son by James Baldwin
Silent Spring by Rachel Carson
The Souls of Black Folk by W.E.B. Du Bois
Self-Reliance by Ralph Waldo Emerson
A Moveable Feast by Ernest Hemingway
The Prince by Niccolo Machiavelli
The Lives of a Cell: Notes of a Biology Watcher by Lewis Thomas
Civil Disobedience by Henry David Thoreau
Up from Slavery by Booker T. Washington
A Room of One's Own by Virginia Woolf

10 Classics for Girls Certain They Will Never Meet Prince Charming

Pride and Prejudice by Jane Austen

Jane Eyre by Charlotte Brontë

Wuthering Heights by Emily Brontë

The Heart Is a Lonely Hunter by Carson McCullers

The Sound of Waves by Yukio Mishima

Gone With the Wind by Margaret Mitchell

Doctor Zhivago by Boris Pasternak

Bonjour Tristesse by Françoise Sagan

Franny and Zooey by J. D. Salinger

A Tree Grows in Brooklyn by Betty Smith

10 Classics for Boys (and Girls) Who Love Action and Hate Long Descriptions of Drawing Rooms and Landscapes

Tarzan of the Apes by Edgar Rice Burroughs

Ender's Game by Orson Scott Card

Riders of the Purple Sage by Zane Grey

The Call of the Wild by Jack London

All Quiet on the Western Front by Erich Maria Remarque

Northwest Passage by Kenneth Roberts

Harry Potter and the Sorcerer's Stone by J. K. Rowling

Ivanhoe by Sir Walter Scott

Kidnapped by Robert Louis Stevenson

The War of the Worlds by H. G. Wells

10 Children's Classics I Can't Imagine Not Having Read

Little Women by Louisa May Alcott

Peter Pan by James Barrie

The Wizard of Oz by L. Frank Baum
Madeline by Ludwig Bemelmans
The Secret Garden by Frances Hodgson Burnett
Alice in Wonderland by Lewis Carroll
The Chronicles of Narnia by C. S. Lewis
A Wrinkle in Time by Madeline L'Engle
Anne of Green Gables by Lucy Maud Montgomery
The Five Little Peppers and How They Grew by Margaret Sidney

10 Classics I Have Never Taught but Look Forward to Teaching Some Day

A Death in the Family by James Agee
Invisible Man by Ralph Ellison
Catch-22 by Joseph Heller
A Farewell to Arms by Ernest Hemingway
Their Eyes Were Watching God by Zora Neale Hurston
Sula by Toni Morrison
Cry, the Beloved Country by Alan Paton
Henry V by William Shakespeare
The Real Thing by Tom Stoppard
The House of Mirth by Edith Wharton

10 Classics from Latin America

Luisa in Realityland by Claribel Alegría
House of the Spirits by Isabel Allende
One Day of Life by Manlio Argueta
Ficciones by Jorge Luis Borges
Blow-Up and Other Stories by Julio Cortázar
Death and the Maiden by Ariel Dorfman
Aura by Carlos Fuentes

The Old Gringo by Carlos Fuentes
The Storyteller by Mario Vargas Llosa
Chronicle of a Death Foretold by Gabriel Garcia Marquez

10 Contemporary Plays That Will One Day Be Classics

W;t by Margaret Edson
"Master Harold" . . . And the Boys by Athol Fugard
Six Degrees of Separation by John Guare
Skylight by David Hare
M Butterfly by David Henry Hwang
Angels in America by Tony Kushner
The Kentucky Cycle by Robert Schenkkan
Arcadia by Tom Stoppard
Fences by August Wilson
Joe Turner's Come and Gone by August Wilson

10 Contemporary Classics from African American Literature

I Know Why the Caged Bird Sings by Maya Angelou
A Lesson Before Dying by Ernest Gaines
Brown Girl, Brownstones by Paule Marshall
The Bluest Eye by Toni Morrison
Jazz by Toni Morrison
Always Outnumbered, Always Outgunned by Walter Mosley
Mama Day by Gloria Naylor
*for colored girls who have considered suicide / when the rainbow
    is enuf* by Ntozake Shange
The Color Purple by Alice Walker
Philadelphia Fire by John Edgar Wideman

10 Contemporary Classics from Native American Literature

The Lone Ranger and Tonto Fistfight in Heaven by Sherman Alexie

The Antelope Wife by Louise Erdrich

The Bingo Palace by Louise Erdrich

A Yellow Raft in Blue Water by Michael Dorris

The Grass Dancer by Susan Power

Grand Avenue by Greg Sarris

Ceremony by Lesley Marmon Silko

The Heirs of Columbus by Gerald Vizenor

Fools Crow by James Welch

Winter in the Blood by James Welch

Works Cited

Arnold, Matthew. *Culture and Anarchy.* Cambridge University Press, 1932.

———. "Buried Life," *Dover Beach and Other Poems.* New York: Dover Publishers, 1994.

Beowulf. Translated by Burton Raffel. New York: Mentor, 1963.

Berthoff, Ann E. "Reclaiming the Active Mind." *College English* 61, no. 6 (July 1999): 671–680.

Birkerts, Sven. *The Gutenberg Elegies, The Fate of Reading in an Electronic Age.* New York: Fawcett Columbine, 1994.

Bloom, Harold. *The Western Canon: The Books and School of the Ages.* New York: Harcourt Brace, 1994.

Booth, Wayne. "The Ethics of Teaching Literature." *College English* 61, no. 1 (September 1998): 41–55.

———. *The Vocation of a Teacher.* The University of Chicago Press, 1988.

Brodsky, Joseph. Nobel Prize acceptance speech, 1987.

California Reading/Language Arts Standards. *California Department of Education, 1999.*

Campbell, Joseph. *The Hero with a Thousand Faces.* Princeton: Princeton University Press, 1973.

Colorado Language Arts Society. *Statement* 33, no. 3 (Summer 1997): 2.

Csikszentmihalyi, Mihaly. *Flow, The Psychology of Optimal Experience.* New York: Harper & Row, 1990.

Cunningham, Michael. *The Hours.* New York: Farrar, Straus and Giroux, 1998.

Cyr, Ellen M., ed. *Cyr's Fourth Reader.* New York: Ginn & Co. Publishers, 1901.

Davies, Robertson. *The Tanner Lectures on Human Values:* Volume 13, 1992. Edited by Grethe B. Peterson. University of Utah Press.

————. *A Voice from the Attic, Essays on the Art of Reading.* New York: Penguin Books, 1988.

Delpit, Lisa. *Other People's Children.* New York: The New Press, 1995.

Denby, David. *Great Books.* New York: Simon & Schuster, 1996.

Dickens, Charles. *Great Expectations.* Oxford: Oxford University Press, 1994.

Dostoevsky, Fyodor. *Crime and Punishment.* Translated by Constance Garnett. New York: Modern Library, 1996.

Eco, Umberto. *Six Walks in a Fictional Woods.* Cambridge, Massachusetts: Harvard University Press, 1994.

Ellison, Ralph. *Invisible Man.* New York: Vintage Books, 1980.

Epstein, Joseph. *The Norton Book of Personal Essays.* New York: W.W. Norton & Company, 1997.

Fishkin, Shelley Fisher. "Don't Judge a Book by Its Author's Color, Rank or Quota Number." *Los Angeles Times,* Friday, March 13, 1998: B9.

Gardner, John. *Grendel.* New York: Vintage Books, 1989.

Gregory, Marshall. "The Many-Headed Hydra of Theory vs. The Unifying Mission of Teaching." *College English* 59, no. 1 (January 1997): 41–58.

Homer. *The Odyssey.* Translated by Albert Cook. New York: W. W. Norton & Company, 1967.

Johnston, Annie Fellows. *The Little Colonel's House Party*. Boston: C. H. Simonds Company, 1921.

Kohn, Alfie. "An Interview with Alfie Kohn." *California English* 1, no. 2 (Winter, 1995): 26–27.

————— *Punished by Rewards*. New York: Houghton Mifflin, 1995.

Mackey, Margaret. "Good-Enough Reading: Momentum and Accuracy in the Reading of Complex Fiction." *Research in the Teaching of English* 31, no. 4 (December 1997): 428-458.

Niles, John D. "Reconceiving Beowulf: Poetry as Social Praxis." *College English* 61, no. 2 (November, 1998): 143–166.

Prose, Francine. "I Know Why the Caged Bird Cannot Read." *Harper's Magazine:* September, 1999.

Quindlen, Anna. *How Reading Changed My Life*. New York: The Library of Contemporary Thought, The Ballantine Publishing Group, 1998.

Rabinowitz, Peter J., and Michael W. Smith. *Authorizing Readers, Resistance and Respect in the Teaching of Literature*. New York: Teachers College Press, 1998.

Rationales for Challenged Books. National Council of Teachers of English in partnership with the International Reading Association. Urbana: National Council of Teachers of English, 1998.

Reid, Louann. "Rationales for Challenged Materials." *Statement 33*, no. 3 (Summer, 1997): 2.

Reid, Louann and Jamie Hayes Neufeld. *Rationales for Teaching Young Adult Literature*. Portland, Maine: Calendar Islands Publishers, 1999.

Rosenberg, Howard. "The Invisible Man Is Alive and Well," *Los Angeles Times / Calendar:* July 25, 1999.

Rosenblatt, Louise M. *Literature As Exploration*. New York: The Modern Language Association, 1983.

Scholes, Robert. *Protocols of Reading*. Yale University Press, 1989.

Shakespeare, William. *The Tragedy of Romeo and Juliet.* New York: The New Folger Library Shakespeare, 1993.

Shelley, Mary. *Frankensein.* New York: Signet, 1994.

Stillman, Peter K. *Introduction to Myth.* Second Edition. Portsmouth, NH: Boynton/Cook Publishers, Inc., 1985.

Stotsky, Sandra. *Losing Our Language.* New York: The Free Press, 1999.

Strickland, James. "What Would You Recommend?" *California English* 3, no. 1 (Fall, 1997): 16–17.

Thoreau, Henry David. "Sunday." *A Week on the Concord and Merrimak Rivers,* edited by Carl F. Hovde, William Howarth, and Elizabeth Hall Witherell. Princeton: Princeton University Press, 1975.

Vygotsky, L. S. *Thought and Language.* E. Hanfmann and G. Vakar, eds. and trans. Cambridge, MA: MIT Press, 1962.

Wharton, Edith. *The Age of Innocence.* New York: Collier Books, 1968.

Wilhelm, Jeffry D. *You Gotta BE the Book.* New York: Teachers College Press, 1997.

Wilson, August. *Fences.* New York: New American Library, 1986.

Woolf, Virginia. *Mrs. Dalloway.* New York: Harcourt Brace and Company, 1997.